Tiger Oak Publications
Editor: Susan Bonne
Editorial Assistant: Beth Dooley
Book Design: Alicia Nammacher
Layout and Design: Julie Szamocki
Publisher: R. Craig Bednar

Land O'Lakes, Inc.
Publisher: Peter Theisen
Publications Manager: Mary Sue Peterson
Food Editor: Cindy Manwarren

Published by Tiger Oak Publications
251 1st Avenue North, Suite 401
Minneapolis, Minnesota 55401

First printing: September 1999
Printed in U.S.A.

ISBN 0-9663558-5-7

TIGER OAK
PUBLICATIONS

Comfort Food

Favorite recipes from the Land O'Lakes Test Kitchens

Land O'Lakes

A History of Fresh Ideas
Over seventy-five years ago, on the rolling grassland dairy farms of Minnesota and Wisconsin, farmers united to form the cooperative creamery that became Land O'Lakes. Driven by a desire to provide consumers with the very best butter possible, they created many innovations in the industry, including making their butter from sweet cream only—an idea that assured butter quality and literally changed America's eating habits.

Home and professional cooks alike responded with enthusiasm, turning to Land O'Lakes for more ideas in using its pure, sweet cream butter. Since 1949, the Land O'Lakes Test Kitchens has been developing recipes used and loved by generations. As we celebrate the Test Kitchens' 50th anniversary, we're proud to bring you this all-new chapter in home cooking with Land O'Lakes.

Fine quality ingredients are key to any efforts in the kitchen. After all, if you are taking the time to cook from scratch, you want delicious results. With fresh-tasting additions like butter, cheese and sour cream, time-tested recipes and your own creativity and skill, cooking and baking become the ultimate simple pleasure. Enjoy!

Questions About Baking?
Since 1990, Land O'Lakes Bakeline operators have been helping home cooks turn out the best baked goods possible. If you have a question about baking or cooking, call

1-800-782-9606

from November 1 through December 24, 8 a.m. to 6 p.m. (CST).

ABOVE: LAND O'LAKES TRUCKS OUTSIDE THE ORGANIZATION'S CHICAGO OFFICES CIRCA 1946 AWAIT THEIR CARGO OF DAIRY PRODUCTS. BELOW: THE BUTTER BOX AT RIGHT WAS THE FIRST TO BEAR THE LAND O'LAKES NAME IN THE MID-1920s; WITHIN A FEW YEARS, IT WAS REDESIGNED TO SHOW MORE OF THE INDIAN MAIDEN.

Chicken Soup & Dumplings, page 24
(On the cover: Simple Shepherd's Pie, page 43)

Contents

Piping hot bowlfuls of Country Chowder, easy Busy Day Chili plus the ultimate in culinary prescriptions, Chicken Soup & Dumplings, buoy the spirit as they warm you right down to your toes.

Winners all, Beef & Onion Stroganoff, East Coast Chicken Cobbler and a collection of other hearty recipes deliver maximum flavor with minimum fuss.

From the cool, sweet crunch of Classic Waldorf Salad to the warm, buttery smoothness of Garlic Mashed Potatoes, taste-of-home accompaniments round out the meal.

Tex-Mex Layered Dip, Oven-Baked Chicken Wings and Philly Cheese Steak Wraps are among our assortment of fun, informal foods. Choose several for a sure-to-please appetizer buffet.

Fragrant with cinnamon and sweet spice, streaked with poppy seeds or fruit, hearty with grains, homemade breads are easy to make and an unexpected pleasure to eat.

In the afternoon with tea, after a hearty supper or on a midnight kitchen raid...almost any time is right for Pumpkin Gingerbread, Caramel Apple Pie and other old-fashioned favorites.

Comfort Food

Home cooking: It's what we all crave when our favorite people gather together, when it's time to mark a family birthday, or when a day has gone badly and home is far away. With the satisfaction of a culinary hug, comfort foods remind us of our happiest moments. These are not designer foods, artfully arranged until they look more like a modern sculpture than a meal. These are homestyle casseroles, hearty stews and soothing sweets, blending the best of the past with our favorite new tastes.

Many of the more than 100 recipes here have been updated to incorporate more varied but readily available ingredients and convenience foods, and all have been carefully tested to ensure success. In addition, many are easily doubled for cook-once, eat-twice convenience. Whether you have leisure enough for slow-simmered stews or your daily reality, with mad dashes to the office or soccer field, requires speedy one-dish specialties, comfort is at hand.

Simple Shepherd's Pie, page 43

New Traditions

Comfort foods still intrigue and entice, soothe and fulfill just as they always have. But the recipes and ingredients have been updated for modern life. These days we're using more spices and herbs, interesting vinegars and a cornucopia of fresh and exotic fare. We may break a few rules, but that's the fun.

Our kitchens and pantries have evolved to match our tastes. There's a microwave on the counter, a bowl of fresh lemons on the table, perhaps pots of herbs and tomatoes ripening on the windowsill. Pasta of all shapes and sizes comprises many a meal, and vegetables have been elevated from side-dish to main-dish fare.

Yet the joy of cooking for family and friends does not require hours in the kitchen—nor is it limited to leisurely weekends. Despite hectic schedules, homemade meals are easier than ever before, thanks to the new accessibility of many flavorful ingredients.

Likewise, you don't need fancy equipment for home cooking at its best. But a few essential tools will speed your tasks and make food preparation the pleasure it was meant to be.

soft touch

Softened butter should give gently when pressed with your finger, but not appear to be melting on the plate. To soften butter quickly, try this tip from Julia Child: strike a stick of cold butter several times with a rolling pin.

COOK'S TOOLS

Knives

The best knives are made of high-carbon steel with "full-tang" blades that run the length of the wood or composite handle and are securely riveted in place. Even if a knife is "dishwasher-safe," blades are easily nicked. Wash good knives by hand, and sharpen them frequently. Invest in the best knives you can afford, care for them well, and they will last you a lifetime. The following knives are the most-used in the kitchen: 8-inch chef's knife, 4- to 6-inch paring knife, and a serrated bread knife.

Pots and Pans

The best cookware is forged of heavy-duty aluminum, stainless steel or copper; many brands are a composite of materials, such as stainless steel over aluminum or enamel on steel. Nonstick coatings, though they wear out over time, are very forgiving and easy to clean.

Skillets and sauté pans. You'll need at least one flat-bottom pan with sides that angle out so you can turn foods easily. A 10-inch skillet or sauté pan is essential; a larger 12-inch pan is nice to have on hand.

Saucepans and pots. An 8-quart stock-pot made of heavy aluminum, stainless steel, or enameled cast iron is essential for soups and stews. In addition, you'll need two or three smaller saucepans; 1-quart, 1½- or 2-quart, and 4-quart are good choices. A Dutch oven is nice for stews and braising. All pans should have lids.

Baking/roasting pans. Start simple. One 9x13-inch metal roasting pan and a 9-inch square metal baking pan will meet most of your needs for roasting a chicken, broiling meat, or baking brownies. Glass or ceramic baking dishes and casseroles, soufflé molds and individual ramekins are other staples in the comfort foods kitchen.

Cookie sheets should be heavy-gauge aluminum with no sides. Overly dark sheets absorb heat and may cause cookie bottoms to over-brown, while cookies made on insulated baking sheets do not brown well.

Bread pans come in a variety of sizes. The recipes in this book call for a 9x5-inch loaf pan or mini 5½x3-inch pans.

Pie pans come in aluminum or glass; those of glass hold more heat and yield a crisp crust. You'll need a 9-inch pan.

Muffin tins of shiny aluminum are best for creating a delicate, light crust, though nonstick is easiest to clean.

Round 9-inch cake pans are used for layer cakes; always have two of the same size.

Tart pans are made of metal or ceramic. Those made of metal come with removable rims for ease in unmolding the tart. Ceramic tart pans are typically one piece. Tart pans are available in a variety of sizes.

Butter Basics

Butter is essential to rich sauces and dense, moist baked goods. For unparalleled taste and texture, use either unsalted or lightly salted Land O'Lakes Butter in everything you make.

Storing butter: For truly memorable treats, remember the three C's of butter storage: clean, cool and covered. To preserve butter's goodness, it should be refrigerated in either a covered container or its original carton. Butter stored in this way is usually good for four months. To freeze, leave butter in its original carton, and place in a resealable freezer bag. Butter will keep up to nine months in the freezer.

When a recipe calls for softened butter, remove butter from the refrigerator and let it stand at room temperature for 30 to 45 minutes. Be careful not to let butter get too soft. Butter should give to gentle pressure, but shouldn't be soft in appearance. Overly soft dough may result in cookies that spread too much while baking.

Springform pans are essential to making cheesecake. The springform pan comes in two pieces. Its sides attach to the bottom and can easily be removed without upsetting the baked cheesecake.

Nonstick bakeware
Nonstick bakeware, though not appropriate for every recipe, is easiest to clean. Wash gently with a sponge and dishsoap; never scour with rough pads or abrasives. The surface scratches easily, so be careful when slicing bars, pies, cakes or breads.

Cutting boards
Plastic boards are easiest to maintain and can go right in your dishwasher. To keep your cutting board from sliding around on the counter, place a damp towel under it.

Measuring Butter		
2 cups = 4 sticks	= 1 pound	
1 cup = 2 sticks	= ½ pound	
½ cup = 1 stick	= ¼ pound	
¼ cup = ½ stick	= 4 tablespoons	

A well-equipped kitchen is a pleasure to cook in. Keep your favorite ingredients in the pantry and your favorite tools close at hand.

Spoons and Spatulas

Wooden spoons don't absorb heat and are good for stovetop stirring, sautéing and stir-frying. They will not scratch nonstick surfaces.

Large stainless spoons are useful for stirring and serving thick stews and casseroles. A slotted spoon is essential for scooping ingredients out of a pot or container, leaving unwanted liquid behind. A deep ladle is perfect for serving soups.

Metal spatulas are a must for flipping foods like pancakes and loosening a cake from its rim. You'll need at least one narrow and one wide spatula.

Whisks are great for light whipping jobs and for keeping sauces smooth.

Measuring tools

Invest in a set of good quality measuring spoons and cups. You'll need a 2-cup glass or plastic cup for liquids plus a set of 1/4- to 1-cup dry measures. Use dry-measuring cups to measure ingredients like flour, salt, sugar; use a liquid measure for milk, cream, stock, and the like. Using the wrong kind of measuring cup, especially when baking, could yield disappointing results.

Straining tools

A colander has many uses in the kitchen, from rinsing fresh fruit to draining pasta; it's nice to have several different sizes. Two fine-meshed strainers, one large and one small, are handy for straining soups or gravies.

Cheese graters are handy for shredding small quantities of cheese or for adding a final touch of cheese to stews, casseroles and pastas.

An instant-read thermometer is the most accurate device for determining when food is done, particularly important when cooking meats.

Metal racks are key for cooling baked goods and roasting (just be sure they fit into your roasting pan.)

A rolling pin is essential for baking cookies, pies and tarts.

A wood rolling pin is lighter, while a ceramic or marble rolling pin stays chilled longer. A stockinet and pastry cloth are also useful in preventing dough from sticking to the pin.

Small electrics

A *food processor* is one of the most important kitchen tools. It can grate, chop, whip, grind, purée, and slice whatever you need in minutes. Just be careful that you don't overprocess foods that are not to be puréed. Use the "pulse" button for control.

Mini choppers, small versions of a food processor, are handy for chopping small quantities of vegetables as well as nuts, herbs and spices.

Electric mixers are standard for whipping egg whites or cream. Few people make a cake today without one.

Another kitchen essential, a *blender* is ideal for puréeing creamy soups and whipping up frothy or frosty drinks.

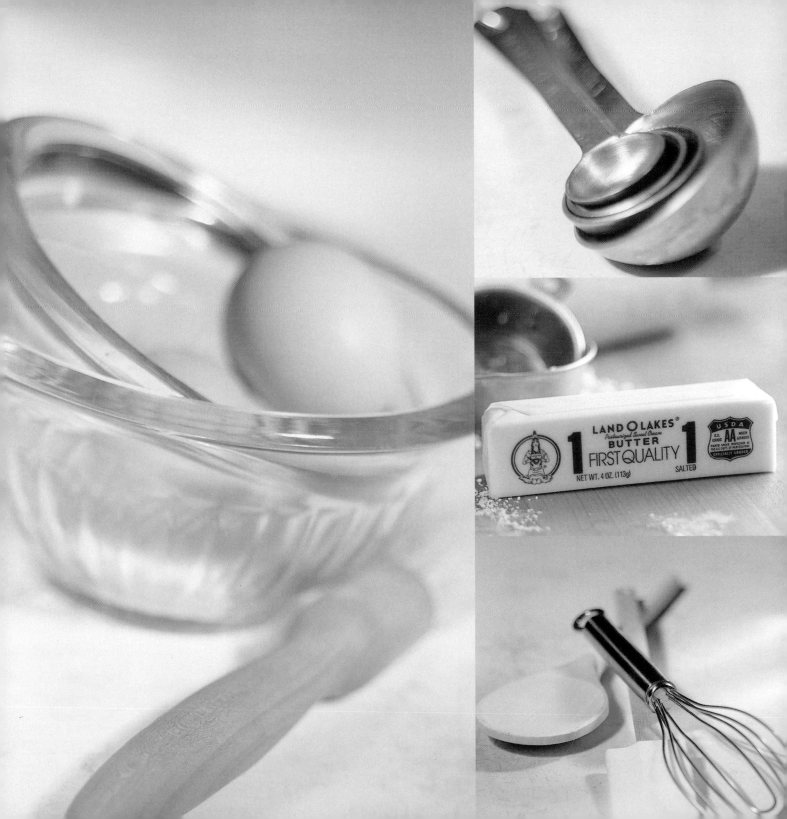

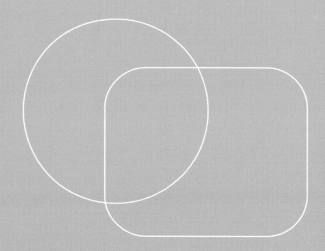

Soups and Stews

Simmering in pots hung over the open hearth, bubbling on the backs of wood-burning stoves, soups and stews are perhaps the original comfort foods. From Country Chowder to Chicken Soup and Dumplings to Savory Vegetable Stew, these hearty suppers can be enjoyed with little more than a good loaf of crusty bread.

Country-Style French Onion Soup

Technique

Lovely as it is, homemade stock is not always a possibility. When relying on canned broth, use low- or no-salt varieties (the seasoned broths tend to be too salty and overpower the flavor of your soup or stew). Adjust seasonings to taste.

The beauty of a soup or stew is in its possibilities. Leftover fresh cooked vegetables, pasta and cheese are natural additions, and open to endless variations. Use your imagination and whatever you have on hand. Here are a few suggestions:

Any leftover cooked pasta or grain (rice, wild rice, brown rice, barley)

Freshly chopped herbs or quick-cooking greens

A drizzle of extra-virgin olive oil over vegetable soups and stews just before serving

Croutons

Shredded or grated cheese for garnish

Country-Style French Onion Soup

Chicken broth and Dijon mustard bring out the mellow, rich flavor of onions.

Preparation time: 15 minutes
Cooking time: 19 minutes
Baking time: 21 minutes

[6 (1¼-cup) servings]

SOUP

2   tablespoons LAND O LAKES® Butter
4   medium (4 cups) onions, sliced ⅛-inch
½   teaspoon finely chopped fresh garlic
2½   cups water
¼   cup chopped fresh parsley
2   (10½-ounce) cans condensed chicken broth
2   tablespoons country-style Dijon mustard
1   teaspoon dried basil leaves
¼   teaspoon pepper
¼   teaspoon dried thyme leaves

CROUTONS

¼   cup LAND O LAKES® Butter
1   teaspoon dried basil leaves
½   teaspoon finely chopped fresh garlic
3   cups cubed 1-inch bread
6   (1-ounce) slices LAND O LAKES® Mozzarella Cheese

1. Heat oven to 400°. Melt 2 tablespoons butter in 3-quart saucepan until sizzling; add onions and ½ teaspoon garlic. Cook over medium heat, stirring occasionally, until onions are tender (7 to 10 minutes).

2. Add all remaining soup ingredients; continue cooking until heated through (12 to 15 minutes).

3. Meanwhile, melt ¼ cup butter in 13x9-inch baking pan in oven (4 to 6 minutes). Stir in 1 teaspoon basil and ½ teaspoon garlic. Add bread cubes; toss to coat. Bake for 10 to 15 minutes, stirring occasionally, until toasted.

4. To serve, pour soup into oven-proof bowls; place *1 slice* cheese in each bowl. Bake for 7 to 10 minutes or until cheese is lightly browned. Serve with croutons.

Nutrition Facts (1 serving): Calories 310; Protein 13 g; Carbohydrate 21 g; Dietary Fiber 3 g; Fat 20 g; Cholesterol 45 mg; Sodium 950 mg

TIP Save time by preparing the croutons the day before you plan to make the soup. Store them, refrigerated, in an airtight container.

All-American Beef Stew

Warm up with a homemade hearty beef stew dinner conveniently made in a slow cooker.

Preparation time: 25 minutes
Cooking time: 5 hours

[6 (1½-cup) servings]

1	tablespoon LAND O LAKES® Butter
1	pound beef stew meat, cut into 1-inch cubes
2	cups vegetable juice cocktail
1	(14½-ounce) can beef broth
2	medium carrots, peeled, sliced 1-inch
2	medium potatoes, peeled, cubed
1	medium onion, cut into 1-inch pieces
1	tablespoon Worcestershire sauce
½	teaspoon garlic salt
½	teaspoon dried thyme leaves
¼	teaspoon dried marjoram leaves
1	bay leaf
1½	cups frozen peas
½	cup water
3	tablespoons all-purpose flour
2	tablespoons red wine *or* beef broth

1. Melt butter in 10-inch skillet until sizzling; add beef cubes. Cook over medium-high heat, stirring occasionally, until browned (5 to 7 minutes).

2. Place beef in slow cooker. Stir in all remaining ingredients *except* peas, water, flour and wine.

3. Cover; cook on High for 5 to 6 hours, or on Low for 8 to 9 hours or until beef is tender. Uncover; remove bay leaf. Stir in peas.

4. Stir together water, flour and wine in small bowl. Slowly stir into beef mixture. Cook on High, stirring occasionally, until thickened (8 to 10 minutes).

Nutrition Facts (1 serving): Calories 330; Protein 23 g; Carbohydrate 23 g; Dietary Fiber 4 g; Fat 16 g; Cholesterol 70 mg; Sodium 930 mg

TIP Add more flour if a thicker stew is desired.

[kitchen notes]

Can't find "stew meat" at your butcher counter? Any beef labeled "chuck" (except ground) will do nicely. Beef chuck, an inexpensive cut of meat from the shoulder, naturally becomes tender as it simmers in water or broth.

Crock of Savory Vegetable Stew

This tomato-based stew is thick with veggies and kielbasa sausage.

Preparation time: 20 minutes
Cooking time: 27 minutes

[6 (1½-cup) servings]

¼	cup LAND O LAKES® Butter
4	medium (2 cups) carrots, sliced
2	stalks (1 cup) celery, sliced
2	medium (1 cup) onions, chopped
4	cups shredded coleslaw mix
1	cup apple juice
½	cup chopped fresh parsley
1	(15-ounce) can tomato sauce
1	(14½-ounce) can diced tomatoes
1	(10¾-ounce) can condensed tomato soup
1	bay leaf
½	teaspoon salt
½	teaspoon dried thyme leaves
¼	teaspoon pepper
1	(16-ounce) package cooked kielbasa, sliced ½-inch

1. Heat butter until sizzling in Dutch oven or 4-quart saucepan; add carrots, celery and onions. Cook over medium heat, stirring occasionally, until vegetables are crisply tender (5 to 7 minutes).

2. Add all remaining ingredients *except* kielbasa. Reduce heat to low. Cover; cook, stirring occasionally, until heated through (12 to 15 minutes).

3. Stir in kielbasa. Continue cooking, stirring occasionally, until heated through (10 to 15 minutes). Remove bay leaf.

Nutrition Facts (1 serving): Calories 440; Protein 14 g; Carbohydrate 32 g; Dietary Fiber 5 g; Fat 30 g; Cholesterol 70 mg; Sodium 2000 mg

Microwave Directions: Combine carrots, celery and onions in 3-quart casserole. Cover; microwave on HIGH, stirring after half the time, until vegetables are crisply tender (4 to 8 minutes). Stir in all remaining ingredients. Cover; microwave on HIGH, stirring after half the time, until slightly thickened and heated through (10 to 15 minutes).

Wild Mushroom Soup with Orzo

The rich flavor of wild mushrooms enhances this easy, elegant turkey soup made with orzo.

Preparation time: 10 minutes
Cooking time: 17 minutes

[6 (1-cup) servings]

2	tablespoons LAND O LAKES® Butter
2	cups chopped fresh wild mushrooms* *or* sliced button mushrooms
¼	cup sliced green onions
1	cup water
2	(14½-ounce) cans reduced sodium chicken broth
2	tablespoons chopped fresh parsley
2	teaspoons chopped fresh thyme leaves**
2	cups cubed cooked turkey
6	ounces (1 cup) uncooked dried rosamarina pasta (orzo) *or* pasta rings
	Salt
	Pepper

1. Melt butter in 3-quart saucepan until sizzling; add mushrooms and green onions. Cook over medium-high heat, stirring occasionally, until mushrooms are tender (3 to 5 minutes). Add water, chicken broth, parsley and thyme. Continue cooking until mixture comes to a full boil (4 to 5 minutes).

2. Reduce heat to medium; add turkey and pasta. Cook, stirring occasionally, until pasta is tender (10 to 12 minutes). Season to taste with salt and pepper.

Nutrition Facts (1 serving): Calories 230; Protein 19 g; Carbohydrate 22 g; Dietary Fiber 1 g; Fat 7 g; Cholesterol 45 mg; Sodium 110 mg

*Substitute shiitake, oyster, portobello, chanterelle and/or crimini mushrooms.

**Substitute ½ teaspoon dried thyme leaves.

Crock of Savory Vegetable Stew

San Francisco Seafood Stew

Serve this quick, easy version of San Francisco's famous seafood stew, Cioppino, with thick slices of sourdough bread.

Preparation time: 20 minutes
Cooking time: 16 minutes

[4 (1½-cup) servings]

1	tablespoon LAND O LAKES® Butter
1	medium (1 cup) green pepper, coarsely chopped
1	medium (½ cup) onion, coarsely chopped
1	cup prepared tomato and basil pasta sauce*
½	cup dry red wine**
2	(8-ounce) bottles clam juice***
2	bay leaves
½	teaspoon dried basil leaves
¼	teaspoon salt
¼	teaspoon coarsely ground pepper
1	pound (about 12) fresh littleneck clams, cleaned
¾-1	pound fresh *or* frozen pollock or other firm white fish, such as haddock *or* cod, cut into 1½-inch slices
½	pound (25-27) fresh *or* frozen medium raw shrimp, shelled, deveined, rinsed, drained

1. Melt butter in 5-quart Dutch oven until sizzling; add green pepper and onion. Cook over medium heat, stirring constantly, until onion is softened (3 to 4 minutes). Add all remaining ingredients *except* clams, fish and shrimp. Continue cooking, stirring occasionally, until heated through (10 to 15 minutes).

2. Add clams and white fish; continue cooking until mixture comes to a boil. Reduce heat to low. Cover; cook 5 minutes. Add shrimp; continue cooking until shrimp turn pink (1 to 2 minutes). Remove bay leaves. Discard any unopened clams.

Nutrition Facts *(1 serving): Calories 410; Protein 58 g; Carbohydrate 18 g; Dietary Fiber 2 g; Fat 9 g; Cholesterol 210 mg; Sodium 1010 mg*

*Substitute 1 cup your favorite tomato-based pasta sauce.

**Substitute ½ cup chicken broth and 1 tablespoon lemon juice.

***Substitute 2 cups chicken broth.

TIP To clean clams, discard any broken-shell or open clams. Place remaining clams in 4-quart Dutch oven. Pour 6 cups water and ⅓ cup vinegar over clams. Let stand 30 minutes; drain. Scrub clams in cold water.

Split Pea Soup

This homemade split pea soup gets a savory kick from smoked ham.

Preparation time: 20 minutes
Cooking time: 1 hour 47 minutes

[6 (1½-cup) servings]

9	cups water
1½	cups chopped celery
2	medium (1 cup) carrots, chopped
2	medium (1 cup) onions, chopped
1½	pounds smoked ham shanks
1	(16-ounce) bag dried green split peas
	Salt
	Pepper

1. Combine all ingredients *except* salt and pepper in Dutch oven. Cook over medium heat until mixture comes to a boil (12 to 14 minutes). Reduce heat to low. Cover; cook, stirring occasionally, until soup begins to thicken (about 1 hour).

2. Remove ham shanks. Continue cooking for 30 minutes.

3. Meanwhile, cut meat off bones; discard bones. Return meat to soup. Cook 5 to 10 minutes longer or until meat is heated through. Season to taste with salt and pepper.

Nutrition Facts *(1 serving): Calories 440; Protein 43 g; Carbohydrate 51 g; Dietary Fiber 21 g; Fat 7 g; Cholesterol 70 mg; Sodium 135 mg*

Fresh parsley is a natural breath freshener. Thoroughly wash parsley and shake off excess moisture, then blot dry with paper towels for easier chopping.

Creamy Corn & Green Chile Soup

This thick, creamy soup features the slow-simmered flavors of roasted chiles, sweet corn and cheese.

Preparation time: 20 minutes
Cooking time: 13 minutes

[4 (1-cup) servings]

2½ cups fat free milk
1   (16-ounce) bag frozen whole
     kernel corn
1   (4-ounce) can chopped
     green chiles
1   (2-ounce) jar diced pimientos,
     drained
3   ounces LAND O LAKES®
     American Cheese, cubed
½   teaspoon salt
     Dash of pepper
2   tablespoons chopped fresh
     parsley

1. Combine ½ *cup* milk, corn, green chilies and pimientos in 2-quart saucepan. Cook over medium-high heat until mixture comes to a boil (3 to 5 minutes). Reduce heat to low. Cover; cook 3 minutes.

2. Add all remaining ingredients *except* parsley. Continue cooking, stirring occasionally, until heated through (10 minutes).

3. Place *half* of corn mixture into 5-cup blender container. Cover; blend until smooth (1 to 2 minutes). Stir in parsley. Repeat with remaining mixture.

Nutrition Facts (1 serving): Calories 240; Protein 14 g; Carbohydrate 34 g; Dietary Fiber 4 g; Fat 8 g; Cholesterol 25 mg; Sodium 990 mg

Minestrone with Sausage

This filling soup offers up the bounty of a country vegetable garden.

Preparation time: 15 minutes
Cooking time: 29 minutes

[8 servings]

4	ounces (1¼ cups) uncooked dried ditalini *or* medium pasta shells
1	tablespoon olive *or* vegetable oil
1	medium (½ cup) onion, chopped
¼	cup chopped fresh basil leaves*
1	teaspoon finely chopped fresh garlic
1	pound chorizo sausage *or* Italian sausage, crumbled
2	medium (1 cup) carrots, sliced
2	medium zucchini, cut into ½-inch pieces
1	(14- to 16-ounce) can whole tomatoes, cut up
2	cups frozen cut green beans
4	(14½-ounce) cans beef broth

  Freshly grated Parmesan cheese

1. Cook ditalini according to package directions. Rinse with hot water; drain. Set aside.

2. Meanwhile, in Dutch oven heat oil; add onion, basil and garlic. Cook over medium high heat, stirring constantly, until onion is soft (3 to 5 minutes). Add sausage. Continue cooking, stirring occasionally, until sausage is browned (9 to 11 minutes). Drain off fat.

3. Stir in all remaining ingredients *except* Parmesan cheese. Continue cooking, stirring occasionally, until vegetables are crisply tender (15 to 20 minutes). Stir in cooked ditalini. Continue cooking, stirring occasionally, until heated through (2 to 3 minutes). Sprinkle each serving with Parmesan cheese.

Nutrition Facts (1 serving): Calories 380; Protein 20 g; Carbohydrate 20 g; Dietary Fiber 0 g; Fat 24 g; Cholesterol 50 mg; Sodium 1460 mg

*Substitute 2 teaspoons dried basil leaves can be substituted for ¼ cup chopped fresh basil leaves.

Snapper Chowder

Fresh garlic and licorice-tinged fennel season this hearty fish chowder.

Preparation time: 10 minutes
Cooking time: 32 minutes

[5 (1⅓-cup) servings]

2	tablespoons LAND O LAKES® Butter
1	large (1 cup) onion, finely chopped
1	teaspoon finely chopped fresh garlic
1	small bulb fennel, finely chopped (1½ cups)
1½	cups water
1	medium (1 cup) red potato, chopped
1	(28-ounce) can diced tomatoes, undrained
1	pound snapper *or* other firm-fleshed fish fillets, cut into 1-inch pieces
¼	teaspoon pepper

  LAND O LAKES® Sour Cream
  Fennel greens

1. Melt butter in large saucepan or Dutch oven until sizzling; add onion, garlic and chopped fennel. Cook over medium-high heat until onion is slightly softened (1 to 2 minutes). Add water, potato and tomatoes. Continue cooking until mixture comes to a boil (4 to 6 minutes). Reduce heat to low. Cook 25 minutes.

2. Add snapper and, if necessary, additional water. Continue cooking until snapper is cooked through (2 to 3 minutes). Garnish with sour cream and fennel greens.

Nutrition Facts (1 serving): Calories 210; Protein 21 g; Carbohydrate 18 g; Dietary Fiber 4 g; Fat 6 g; Cholesterol 45 mg; Sodium 380 mg

TIP Snapper cooks quickly; be careful to not over-cook.

Minestrone with Sausage

Chicken Soup & Dumplings

Homemade dumplings and soup provide comfort on a chilly night.

Preparation time: 20 minutes
Cooking time: 2 hours 30 minutes

[6 (1-cup) servings]

SOUP

8	cups water
2	pounds chicken wings
2	medium (1 cup) onions, chopped
1	teaspoon salt
3/4	teaspoon pepper
1	bay leaf
3	carrots (1 1/2 cups), sliced
2	stalks (1 cup) celery, chopped
1/2	teaspoon garlic salt

DUMPLINGS

1	cup all-purpose flour
1 1/2	teaspoons baking powder
1/4	teaspoon salt
2	tablespoons cold LAND O LAKES® Butter
1/2	cup milk
3	tablespoons chopped fresh parsley

1. Place water, chicken wings, *1/2 cup* onion, 1 teaspoon salt, *1/2 teaspoon* pepper and bay leaf in Dutch oven. Cover; cook over high heat until mixture comes to a full boil (10 to 15 minutes). Reduce heat to low. Cover; cook until chicken is tender and comes off the bone (1 to 1 1/2 hours).

2. Remove chicken from broth. Cool chicken slightly; remove from bones. Discard bones and skin. Strain broth.

3. Return chicken and broth to Dutch oven. Add remaining onions, 1/4 teaspoon pepper and all remaining soup ingredients. Increase heat to high. Cook until mixture comes to a boil (10 to 15 minutes). Reduce heat to low. Cook 5 to 10 minutes or until heated through.

4. Meanwhile, stir together flour, baking powder and 1/4 teaspoon salt in small bowl; cut in butter until mixture is crumbly. Stir in milk and parsley. Drop mixture by rounded teaspoonfuls onto boiling soup. Cover; cook 10 minutes. Remove cover; continue cooking 10 minutes.

Nutrition Facts (1 serving): Calories 490; Protein 32 g; Carbohydrate 25 g; Dietary Fiber 3 g; Fat 29 g; Cholesterol 130 mg; Sodium 870 mg

Tomato Barley Soup

Fill your kitchen with the aroma of garlic and onions.

Preparation time: 20 minutes
Cooking time: 25 minutes

[6 (1-cup) servings]

1	tablespoon LAND O LAKES® Butter
2	medium (1 cup) carrots, sliced 1/4-inch
2	medium (1 cup) onions, chopped
1	tablespoon finely chopped fresh garlic
2 1/2	cups water
1/2	cup uncooked quick barley*
2	(14 1/2-ounce) cans diced tomatoes
1	(14 1/2-ounce) can chicken broth
1/4	teaspoon pepper

1. Melt butter in 2-quart saucepan until sizzling; add carrots, onions and garlic. Cook over medium heat, stirring occasionally, until vegetables are crisply tender (5 to 7 minutes).

2. Meanwhile, combine all remaining ingredients in 3-quart saucepan. Cook over medium heat until mixture comes to a full boil (3 to 5 minutes). Add vegetable mixture; return to a boil (2 to 3 minutes). Reduce heat to low. Cover; cook until barley is tender (15 to 20 minutes).

Nutrition Facts (1 serving): Calories 140; Protein 5 g; Carbohydrate 25 g; Dietary Fiber 5 g; Fat 3 g; Cholesterol 5 mg; Sodium 460 mg

*Substitute 1/2 cup regular barley and cook until barley is tender (35 to 40 minutes).

Minnesota Wild Rice Soup

Serve this Midwestern classic on a cold winter evening with good bread and a green salad.

Preparation time: 20 minutes
Cooking time: 61 minutes

[8 (1½-cup) servings]

11	cups water
1	cup uncooked wild rice
½	cup LAND O LAKES® Butter
1	large (1½ cups) onion, coarsely chopped
1	(8-ounce) package fresh mushrooms, sliced
1	cup all-purpose flour
3	tablespoons instant chicken bouillon granules
2	cups chopped cooked chicken
1	cup half-and-half
	Salt
	Pepper

1. Combine *4 cups* water and wild rice in 2-quart saucepan. Cook over medium-high heat until water comes to a boil (4 to 5 minutes). Reduce heat to low. Cook until rice is tender and liquid is absorbed (40 to 50 minutes). Set aside.

2. Melt butter in 4-quart Dutch oven until sizzling; add onion and mushrooms. Cook over medium heat, stirring occasionally, until onion is tender (4 to 5 minutes). Add remaining water and bouillon granules.

3. Stir together 1 cup soup mixture and flour in small bowl. Stir into remaining soup mixture. Cook, stirring occasionally, until soup is thickened (8 to 10 minutes). Boil 1 minute. Add cooked rice and chicken. Continue cooking until heated through (4 to 5 minutes).

4. Add half-and-half, continue cooking until heated through (1 to 2 minutes). (DO NOT BOIL.) Season to taste with salt and pepper.

Nutrition Facts (1 serving): Calories 350; Protein 16 g; Carbohydrate 31 g; Dietary Fiber 2 g; Fat 18 g; Cholesterol 70 mg; Sodium 410 mg

TIP For thinner soup, add 1 cup half-and-half or milk.

[kitchen notes]

A delicacy once difficult to find outside the Midwest, wild rice is native to the Great Lakes region and must be harvested by hand. Technically not a rice at all, wild rice is actually the seed of a marsh grass that thrives in cold climates. With a chewy texture and nutty flavor, wild rice is heartier than either white or brown rice, though it blends well with either variety. Wash wild rice carefully before cooking.

Southwest Black Bean Soup

Green chiles and red pepper lend zest to this easy dinnertime offering.

Preparation time: 15 minutes
Cooking time: 12 minutes

[6 (1-cup) servings]

2	tablespoons vegetable oil
1	medium (½ cup) onion, chopped
1	medium red pepper, chopped
2	stalks (1 cup) celery, sliced
1	(15- to 16-ounce) can Mexican-style *or* stewed tomatoes
1	(14½-ounce) can beef or vegetable broth
2	(15-ounce) cans black beans, rinsed, drained
1	(4-ounce) can chopped green chilies
2	tablespoons dry sherry, if desired
1	teaspoon ground cumin
	LAND O LAKES® Sour Cream, if desired

1. Heat oil in 4-quart saucepan; add onion, red pepper and celery. Cook over medium heat, stirring occasionally, until crisply tender (2 to 3 minutes).

2. Add all remaining ingredients *except* sour cream. Reduce heat to medium-low. Cook, stirring occasionally, until heated through and flavors are blended (10 to 15 minutes).

3. To serve, top each serving with dollop of sour cream, if desired.

Nutrition Facts (1 serving): Calories 210; Protein 11 g; Carbohydrate 32 g; Dietary Fiber 7 g; Fat 5 g; Cholesterol 0 mg; Sodium 1180 mg

TIP Mexican-style stewed tomatoes are spiced with chili powder, and often cilantro for a little extra kick. Look for them under several popular brand names in the Mexican foods aisle of the supermarket.

Country Chowder with Pasta & Cheese

Broccoli, cauliflower and carrots give this quick dish great texture and color.

Preparation time: 5 minutes
Cooking time: 16 minutes

[6 (1⅓-cup) servings]

1	(14½-ounce) can chicken broth
1	medium (½ cup) onion, chopped
4	ounces (1¼ cups) uncooked dried rotini (corkscrew *or* pasta twists)
2	cups small broccoli florets
2	cups small cauliflower florets
1	medium carrot, cut into julienne strips
1½	cups milk
12	ounces sliced LAND O LAKES® American Cheese, quartered
8	ounces deli turkey, chopped

1. Place chicken broth and onion in 4-quart saucepan. Cook over medium-high heat until mixture comes to a full boil (3 to 5 minutes).

2. Add rotini. Continue cooking, stirring occasionally, until pasta is tender (6 to 8 minutes). Stir in vegetables, milk, cheese and turkey. Continue cooking, stirring occasionally, until cheese is melted and vegetables are tender (7 to 10 minutes).

Nutrition Facts (1 serving): Calories 390; Protein 27 g; Carbohydrate 26 g; Dietary Fiber 3 g; Fat 20 g; Cholesterol 75 mg; Sodium 1670 mg

TIP For a delicious vegetarian version of this soup, simply omit the turkey.

Southwest Black Bean Soup

Curried Meat & Vegetable Stew

Curry powder and raisins give a Middle-Eastern flavor to this hearty stew.

Preparation time: 25 minutes
Cooking time: 34 minutes

[6 (1 1/3-cup) servings]

MEAT

1	tablespoon LAND O LAKES® Butter
1	pound boneless pork *or* lamb, cut into 1/2-inch pieces
1	medium (1/2 cup) onion, chopped
2	teaspoons curry powder

STOCK

1	cup chopped parsnip
1/4	cup raisins
2	medium (1 cup) carrots, chopped
1	stalk (1/2 cup) celery, chopped
2	(14 1/2-ounce) cans low-sodium chicken broth
1	(14 1/2-ounce) can tomatoes, cut-up
2	tablespoons chopped fresh cilantro
1	tablespoon lemon juice
1/4	teaspoon ground cinnamon
1/4	teaspoon pepper

PASTA

3 1/2	ounces (1/2 cup) uncooked dried rosamarina pasta (orzo)

Plain yogurt, if desired

1. Melt butter in 3-quart saucepan until sizzling; add pork, onion and curry powder. Cook over medium-high heat, stirring occasionally, until browned (5 to 7 minutes). Drain off fat.

2. Stir in all stock ingredients. Continue cooking until mixture comes to a full boil (6 to 8 minutes). Reduce heat to low. Cover; continue cooking, stirring occasionally, 10 minutes.

3. Stir in pasta. Cover; continue cooking, stirring occasionally, until pork and pasta are tender (13 to 15 minutes). Top individual servings with dollop of yogurt, if desired.

Nutrition Facts (1 serving): Calories 330; Protein 27 g; Carbohydrate 30 g; Dietary Fiber 4 g; Fat 12 g; Cholesterol 70 mg; Sodium 510 mg

Catalán Fish Stew

Thick with potatoes, peppers and artichokes, this stew is flavorful yet low in fat.

Preparation time: 15 minutes
Cooking time: 25 minutes

[4 (2-cup) servings]

1/2	pound small new red potatoes, quartered
1	tablespoon olive *or* vegetable oil
1	(16-ounce) package frozen pepper stir-fry vegetable combination
2	teaspoons purchased minced garlic
1	(14 1/2-ounce) can Italian-style diced tomatoes
1	(14-ounce) can artichoke hearts, drained, quartered
1	pound halibut *or* swordfish steak, cut into 3/4-inch pieces
3/4	cup chopped fresh parsley
	Salt
	Pepper

1. Place potatoes and enough water to cover in 1 1/2-quart saucepan. Cook over high heat until water comes to a boil (8 to 10 minutes). Reduce heat to low. Cook 10 minutes. Drain.

2. Meanwhile, heat oil in Dutch oven; add pepper mixture and garlic. Cook over medium-high heat 3 minutes. Stir in tomatoes and artichokes; continue cooking 1 minute.

3. Add potatoes and fish; continue cooking until fish flakes with fork (4 minutes). Stir in parsley. Season with salt and pepper to taste.

Nutrition Facts (1 serving): Calories 310; Protein 30 g; Carbohydrate 32 g; Dietary Fiber 9 g; Fat 7 g; Cholesterol 35 mg; Sodium 650 mg

The leaf of the bay laurel tree is one of the most ancient of culinary herbs. Laurel was revered by Greeks and Romans alike, who regarded it as a symbol of honor and celebration.

Vegetable Chicken Pasta Stew

A medley of vegetables and fresh-tasting seasonings give chicken and pasta a new spin.

Preparation time: 30 minutes
Cooking time: 28 minutes

[8 (1¼-cup) servings]

1	tablespoon LAND O LAKES® Butter
2	medium (1 cup) onions, chopped
2	stalks (1 cup) celery, sliced
1	teaspoon finely chopped fresh garlic
3	(14½-ounce) cans low-sodium chicken broth
1	(14½-ounce) can diced tomatoes
2	medium (1 cup) carrots, sliced ¼-inch
1	medium (1 cup) potato, chopped ½-inch
1	small (1 cup) rutabaga, peeled, chopped ½-inch
2	bay leaves
1½	teaspoons dried marjoram leaves
½	teaspoon salt
¼	teaspoon pepper
⅛	teaspoon caraway seed
4	ounces (1 cup) uncooked dried ditalini pasta *or* small pasta shells
1½	cups cubed ½-inch cooked chicken

1. Melt butter in Dutch oven until sizzling; add onions, celery and garlic. Cook over medium heat, stirring occasionally, until onions are softened (5 to 8 minutes).

2. Add all remaining ingredients *except* pasta and chicken; continue cooking, stirring occasionally, until carrots are just tender (15 to 20 minutes).

3. Add pasta and chicken; continue cooking, stirring occasionally, until pasta is tender (8 to 10 minutes). Remove bay leaves.

Nutrition Facts (1 serving): Calories 220; Protein 14 g; Carbohydrate 30 g; Dietary Fiber 3 g; Fat 4 g; Cholesterol 25 mg; Sodium 310 mg

TIP The herb marjoram is a member of the mint family. Its flavor is similar to oregano, but sweeter and milder. Marjoram enhances almost any meat dish and pairs well with root vegetables. Also try marjoram in marinades and herb butters.

Busy Day Chili

A quick and richly flavored dish, this chili is made with turkey or ground beef.

Preparation time: 15 minutes
Cooking time: 10 minutes

[8 (1-cup) servings]

2   teaspoons vegetable oil
1   pound lean ground turkey
     or ground beef
1   medium onion, chopped
1   medium yellow pepper,
     chopped
1   (1.25-ounce) package chili
     seasoning mix
4   cups vegetable juice cocktail
2   (14.5-ounce) cans diced chili-
     style chunky tomatoes
1   (16-ounce) can dark red kidney
     beans
½   cup LAND O LAKES® Sour
     Cream
2   ounces (½ cup)
     LAND O LAKES® Cheddar
     Cheese, shredded

1. In Dutch oven heat oil; add turkey, onion and yellow pepper. Cook over medium-high heat, stirring occasionally, until turkey is no longer pink and vegetables are tender (5 to 8 minutes).

2. Stir in chili seasoning mix. Stir in all remaining ingredients *except* sour cream and cheese. Reduce heat to medium-low. Cook, stirring occasionally, until chili comes to a boil (5 to 7 minutes).

3. To serve, dollop each serving with *1 tablespoon* sour cream; sprinkle with *1 tablespoon* cheese.

Nutrition Facts (1 serving): Calories 270; Protein 17 g; Carbohydrate 26 g; Dietary Fiber 5 g; Fat 11 g; Cholesterol 60 mg; Sodium 1670 mg

Spicy Garbanzo Bean Soup

Tortilla chips are a natural accompaniment to this main dish soup.

Preparation time: 10 minutes
Cooking time: 18 minutes

[6 (1⅓-cup) servings]

2   cups frozen diced hash-brown
     potatoes
1½   cups water
2   (5.5-ounce) cans spicy hot
     tomato vegetable juice*
1   (15-ounce) can garbanzo beans
     (chickpeas), rinsed, drained,
1   (11-ounce) can whole kernel
     corn with red and green
     peppers, drained
1   (4-ounce) can chopped
     green chilies, drained
1   teaspoon ground cumin
½   teaspoon garlic salt

     LAND O LAKES® Chedarella
     Cheese, shredded
     Chopped fresh cilantro leaves,
     if desired

1. Combine all ingredients *except* cheese in 3-quart saucepan. Cook over medium-high heat until mixture comes to a boil (8 to 10 minutes). Continue cooking until potatoes are fork tender (10 to 13 minutes).

2. Top with cheese. Garnish with chopped cilantro, if desired.

Nutrition Facts (1 serving): Calories 200; Protein 7 g; Carbohydrate 42 g; Dietary Fiber 6 g; Fat 1.5 g; Cholesterol 0 mg; Sodium 800 mg

*Substitute 1 (11-ounce) can plain vegetable juice cocktail.

Busy Day Chili

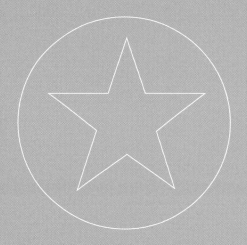

Main Dishes

Comfort meets convenience in the humble guise of the casserole, skillet dinner and one-dish meal. Most of these entrees can be prepared and assembled in under half an hour, then left to bake in the oven or simmer on the stovetop with no further help from you until serving time.

Earth Risotto

Technique

It's not always necessary to preheat the oven, especially for foods that will cook for more than an hour, such as roasts and casseroles. However, for recipes calling for shorter baking times (cookies, muffins, etc.) the oven should preheat about 10 minutes.

To cut fat and calories from dishes without sacrificing taste, try using reduced fat sour cream. LAND O LAKES® Light Sour Cream or No Fat Sour Cream may be used interchangeably with regular sour cream in both sweet and savory recipes.

Remember that pre-cut foods like boneless meats, pre-chopped vegetables and refrigerated mashed or shredded potatoes can be a busy cook's secret friend. They may cost a little more, but the time and effort you save makes them well worth it.

Earth Risotto

Butternut squash and raisins add a touch of sweetness to this rich-tasting entree.

Preparation time: 15 minutes
Cooking time: 28 minutes

[4 (1¼-cup) servings]

1	tablespoon LAND O LAKES® Butter
½	cup finely chopped onion
1	cup uncooked arborio rice
3-3½	cups vegetable broth *or* chicken broth
¼	cup white wine *or* apple juice
1	medium (2 cups) butternut squash, quartered, seeded, peeled, cubed ½-inch
1	medium (1 cup) red apple, chopped
¼	cup raisins Salt, if desired

1. Melt butter in 10-inch skillet until sizzling; add onion. Cook over medium heat, stirring occasionally, until softened (4 to 5 minutes). Add rice; continue cooking, stirring constantly, 2 minutes. Reduce heat to medium-low; slowly add *1½ cups* broth and wine. Cover; cook 10 minutes.

2. Uncover; add squash and apples. Continue cooking, adding remaining broth *½ cup* at a time and stirring occasionally, until most of liquid is absorbed, and rice is tender and creamy (4 to 5 minutes for each addition of broth, totaling 12 to 15 minutes).

3. Reduce heat to low; add raisins. Cook until heated through (1 to 2 minutes). Season with salt, if desired.

Nutrition Facts (1 serving): Calories 340; Protein 9 g; Carbohydrate 68 g; Dietary Fiber 6 g; Fat 4.5 g; Cholesterol 10 mg; Sodium 620 mg

TIP Butternut squash is a large winter squash variety that is gourd-shaped, with a yellow-to-tan rind and orange flesh. To make peeling the squash easier, first cut it into several large chunks. Peel with a sturdy vegetable peeler or paring knife, then cut into ½-inch cubes as directed.

Beef & Onion Stroganoff

Create this skillet main dish for an easy weeknight meal.

Preparation time: 20 minutes
Cooking time: 32 minutes

[6 servings]

3	tablespoons LAND O LAKES® Butter
2	medium onions, cut into ¼-inch slices
1	(8-ounce) package fresh mushrooms, sliced
4	teaspoons finely chopped fresh garlic
1	pound boneless beef sirloin, cut into bite-size strips
1¾	cups water
¼	cup ketchup
2	teaspoons instant beef bouillon granules
½	teaspoon salt
⅓	cup flour
1	cup LAND O LAKES® Sour Cream
6	cups hot cooked noodles

1. Melt butter in 12-inch skillet until sizzling; add onions. Cook over medium heat, stirring occasionally, until onions are softened (4 to 5 minutes). Stir in mushrooms and garlic. Continue cooking 5 minutes. Remove mixture with slotted spoon. Set aside.

2. Place beef in same skillet. Cook over medium-high heat until browned (6 to 8 minutes).

3. Stir in *1 cup* water, ketchup, bouillon granules and salt. Continue cooking until mixture just comes to a boil (2 to 3 minutes). Reduce heat to medium-low. Cook 10 minutes.

4. Stir together remaining water and flour with wire whisk in small bowl until smooth. Stir into beef mixture. Cook until mixture comes to a full boil (2 to 3 minutes). Boil 1 minute.

5. Add onion mixture and sour cream. Continue cooking until mixture is heated through (3 to 4 minutes). Serve over hot cooked noodles.

Nutrition Facts (1 serving): Calories 510; Protein 28 g; Carbohydrate 56 g; Dietary Fiber 3 g; Fat 19 g; Cholesterol 135 mg; Sodium 640 mg

---

[kitchen notes]

Risotto is a classic northern Italian dish that is made with short-grain rice such as arborio rice simmered in stock that is added to the rice ½ cup at a time so that the liquid is absorbed slowly. The high-starch kernels of arborio rice are shorter than other rices, and the increased starch lends risotto its uniquely creamy texture.

Midwest Macaroni & Cheese

Simple and satisfying, this updated favorite comes together in about 20 minutes.

Preparation time: 15 minutes
Cooking time: 5 minutes

[4 (1-cup) servings]

6   ounces (1½ cups) uncooked dried elbow macaroni
1   cup milk
12   ounces (3 cups) LAND O LAKES® American, Sharp American *or* American & Swiss Cheese, cut into ½-inch cubes
½   cup coarsely crushed seasoned croutons

1. Cook macaroni according to package directions. Drain.

2. Combine cooked macaroni, milk and cheese in medium saucepan. Cook over medium heat, stirring occasionally, until cheese is melted (5 to 6 minutes).

3. Spoon macaroni into individual serving dishes; sprinkle with crushed croutons.

Nutrition Facts (1 serving): Calories 550; Protein 27 g; Carbohydrate 42 g; Dietary Fiber 2 g; Fat 31 g; Cholesterol 85 mg; Sodium 1400 mg

TIP Stir in 1 cup cooked peas *or* chopped broccoli *or* 1 cup cubed deli ham.

Easy Lasagna

This 50-minute lasagna has all the flavor of one that takes half a day to prepare.

Preparation time: 20 minutes
Baking time: 30 minutes

[9 servings]

FILLING
1   pound Italian sausage
8   ounces (2 cups) LAND O LAKES® Mozzarella Cheese, shredded
1   cup ricotta cheese
1   egg
1   teaspoon Italian seasoning*

SAUCE
1   (26- to 28-ounce) jar spaghetti sauce

NOODLES
6   no-boil *or* precooked lasagna noodles**

1. Heat oven to 350°. Place Italian sausage in 10-inch skillet. Cook over medium-high heat, stirring occasionally, until sausage is no longer pink (7 to 9 minutes). Drain off fat.

2. Stir together cooked sausage, *1 cup* mozzarella cheese and all remaining filling ingredients in small bowl.

3. Spoon about *½ cup* spaghetti sauce into ungreased 8-inch square baking pan. Place *2* lasagna noodles over spaghetti sauce. Spoon about *⅓* filling over lasagna noodles. Spoon about *¾ cup* spaghetti sauce over filling; top with *2* lasagna noodles, *⅓* filling and about *¾ cup* spaghetti sauce. Repeat layers with remaining ingredients.

4. Cover with aluminum foil. Bake for 30 to 40 minutes or until heated through. Sprinkle with remaining mozzarella cheese. Cover; let stand 5 minutes or until cheese is melted.

Nutrition Facts (1 serving): Calories 400; Protein 22 g; Carbohydrate 31 g; Dietary Fiber 3 g; Fat 21 g; Cholesterol 75 mg; Sodium 920 mg

*Substitute ¼ teaspoon *each* dried oregano leaves, dried marjoram leaves and dried basil leaves and ⅛ teaspoon rubbed sage.

**Substitute 9 uncooked dried lasagna noodles. Cook according to package directions. Drain.

Midwest Macaroni & Cheese

Short-Cut Chicken Jambalaya

The rice cooks right in the pot for a quick, Southern-style dinner.

Preparation time: 10 minutes
Cooking time: 18 minutes

[6 (1¼-cup) servings]

¼   cup LAND O LAKES® Butter
1   cup cubed (½-inch) ham
¾   cup chopped onion
2   tablespoons all-purpose flour
1½   cups water
1   (14½-ounce) can stewed
       tomatoes, undrained
2   bay leaves
1   teaspoon Cajun seasoning
½   teaspoon salt
2   cups uncooked instant rice
1   (15-ounce) package chicken
       tenders

1. Melt butter in 12-inch skillet until sizzling; add ham and onion. Cook over medium heat, stirring occasionally, until onion is softened (5 to 7 minutes). Stir in flour until smooth. Add water, tomatoes, bay leaves, Cajun seasoning and salt. Continue cooking, stirring occasionally, until mixture comes to a boil (3 to 5 minutes).

2. Stir in rice and chicken. Cover; continue cooking, stirring occasionally, until rice is tender and chicken is no longer pink (10 to 15 minutes). Remove bay leaf.

Nutrition Facts (1 serving): Calories 330; Protein 25 g; Carbohydrate 35 g; Dietary Fiber 2 g; Fat 10 g; Cholesterol 75 mg; Sodium 890 mg

Deep-Dish Turkey Pot Pie

This special pot pie has a buttery, flaky crust and is filled with turkey and vegetables.

Preparation time: 45 minutes
Baking time: 1 hour

[6 servings]

CRUST

2   cups all-purpose flour
¼   teaspoon salt
⅔   cup cold LAND O LAKES®
       Butter
4-6   tablespoons cold water

FILLING

¼   cup milk
1   (10¾-ounce) can condensed
       cream of chicken soup
3   cups cubed 1-inch cooked
       turkey *or* chicken
4   ounces (1 cup)
       LAND O LAKES® Cheddar
       Cheese, shredded
1   (16-ounce) package frozen
       vegetable combination
       (broccoli, cauliflower, carrots)
1   (15-ounce) can whole potatoes,
       drained, quartered
½   teaspoon dried thyme leaves
1   egg, slightly beaten
1   tablespoon water

1. Heat oven to 375°. Stir together flour and salt in large bowl; cut in butter until crumbly. Mix in cold water with fork until flour is just moistened. Divide dough into thirds. Wrap one-third dough in plastic food wrap; set aside.

2. Roll out remaining two-thirds dough on lightly floured surface into 14-inch circle. Gently fit into 2-quart deep-dish casserole. Trim pastry to 1-inch from edge of casserole; set aside.

3. Combine milk and soup in large bowl; mix well. Add all remaining filling ingredients *except* egg and 1 tablespoon water. Spoon into prepared pie crust.

4. Roll reserved dough on lightly floured surface into 10-inch circle. Cut into 8 (1-inch) strips with sharp knife or pastry wheel. Place 4 strips, 1 inch apart, across filling in casserole. Place remaining 4 strips, 1 inch apart, at right angles to strips already in place; trim strips. Fold trimmed edge of bottom pastry over strips; build up an edge. Crimp or flute edges to seal.

5. Combine egg and 1 tablespoon water in small bowl; lightly brush crust with egg mixture. Bake for 60 to 70 minutes or until golden brown. Let stand 10 minutes before serving.

Nutrition Facts (1 serving): Calories 670; Protein 34 g; Carbohydrate 51 g; Dietary Fiber 5 g; Fat 36 g; Cholesterol 175 mg; Sodium 1100 mg

Pasta is comfort food versatility: hearty and filling, it can be dressed simply in butter and a shake of Parmesan, or tossed with whatever sauces and extras your heart desires.

Mexican Manicotti

Mexican and Italian cuisines come together in this savory meatless meal.

Preparation time: 20 minutes
Baking time: 45 minutes

[5 servings]

12   ounces (3 cups)
      LAND O LAKES® Monterey
      Jack Cheese, shredded
1   (16-ounce) can refried beans
10   uncooked dried manicotti pasta
      tubes
1   cup water
1   (10-ounce) can mild enchilada
      sauce
1   (8-ounce) can tomato sauce
¼   cup sliced green onions
¼   cup sliced pitted ripe olives

      LAND O LAKES® Sour Cream,
      if desired

1. Heat oven to 375°. Combine *1½ cups* cheese and refried beans in medium bowl. Stuff uncooked pasta tubes with cheese mixture, pressing firmly into shells.

2. Meanwhile, combine water, enchilada sauce and tomato sauce in 4-cup glass measure. Microwave on HIGH until mixture is steaming hot (5 to 6 minutes). Pour about half of sauce into 12x8-inch baking dish. Place uncooked stuffed tubes in dish, turning each to coat with sauce; top with remaining sauce.

3. Cover; bake for 20 minutes. Turn shells over. Continue baking, covered, for 20 minutes. Uncover; top with remaining cheese. Continue baking until cheese is melted (4 to 5 minutes).

4. Sprinkle with green onions and olives. Dollop with sour cream, if desired. Let stand 5 minutes before serving.

Nutrition Facts (1 serving): Calories 570; Protein 26 g; Carbohydrate 49 g; Dietary Fiber 7 g; Fat 30 g; Cholesterol 90 mg; Sodium 1190 mg

TIP Pasta tubes can be stuffed up to 12 hours ahead. Cover; refrigerate. Prepare and bake as directed above.

Delta-Style Kielbasa & Orzo

This Louisiana take on red beans and rice is ready to eat in under 25 minutes.

Preparation time: 5 minutes
Cooking time: 17 minutes

[6 servings]

1	pound kielbasa sausage, cut diagonally into ¼-inch slices
1	(15-ounce) can red beans, rinsed, drained
1	(14½-ounce) can chicken broth
1	(14½-ounce) can diced tomatoes
8	ounces (1¼ cups) uncooked dried rosamarina pasta (orzo) *or* pasta rings
2	medium green, red *and/or* yellow peppers, cut into strips
1	medium (½ cup) onion, chopped
1	tablespoon chopped fresh thyme leaves*

1. Spray 4-quart Dutch oven with no stick cooking spray; add sausage. Cook over medium-high heat, stirring occasionally, until sausage is browned (4 to 5 minutes).

2. Add all remaining ingredients. Reduce heat to medium. Cover; cook, stirring occasionally, until pasta is just tender (13 to 15 minutes).

Nutrition Facts *(1 serving): Calories 470; Protein 21 g; Carbohydrate 46 g; Dietary Fiber 6 g; Fat 22 g; Cholesterol 50 mg; Sodium 1270 mg*

*Substitute 1 teaspoon dried thyme leaves.

VARIATION Use 8 ounces kielbasa and 8 ounces peeled uncooked shrimp; add shrimp during last 5 minutes of cooking.

Fish and Vegetable Skillet Dinner

Hearty vegetables and fish comprise this easy stovetop entree.

Preparation time: 10 minutes
Cooking time: 14 minutes

[4 servings]

2	tablespoons LAND O LAKES® Roasted Garlic Butter with Olive Oil*
1	tablespoon lemon juice
1	teaspoon dried dill weed
½	teaspoon salt
½	teaspoon pepper
3-4	medium (2 cups) carrots, sliced ¼-inch thick
2	medium (2 cups) potatoes, thinly sliced
1	medium onion, cut into rings
1	pound fresh *or* frozen cod *or* halibut fillets, thawed
2	medium tomatoes, cut into 1-inch pieces

1. Melt garlic butter in 12-inch skillet until sizzling; stir in lemon juice, dill weed, salt and pepper. Add carrots, potato and onion. Cover; cook over medium-high heat, stirring occasionally, until vegetables are crisply tender (7 to 10 minutes).

2. Add fish, arranging vegetables on top. Cover; continue cooking 5 minutes. Sprinkle tomato over fish.

3. Cover; continue cooking until tomato is heated through and fish flakes with a fork (2 to 3 minutes).

Microwave Directions: Microwave garlic butter on HIGH in 13x9-inch baking dish (50 to 60 seconds); stir in salt, dill weed, pepper and lemon juice. Add carrots, potato and onion. Cover; microwave on HIGH, stirring after half the time, until vegetables are crisply tender (8 to 10 minutes). Add fish, arranging vegetables on top. Cover; microwave on HIGH 3 minutes. Turn dish ¼ turn; sprinkle tomato over fish. Cover; microwave on HIGH until fish flakes with a fork (2 to 3 minutes).

Nutrition Facts *(1 serving): Calories 230; Protein 23 g; Carbohydrate 22 g; Dietary Fiber 4 g; Fat 7 g; Cholesterol 60 mg; Sodium 420 mg*

*Substitute 2 tablespoons LAND O LAKES® Butter and 2 teaspoons finely chopped fresh garlic.

Delta-Style Kielbasa & Orzo

East Coast Chicken Cobbler

Tangy cheddar cheese adds zip to the savory biscuit topping on this easy-to-fix pot pie.

Preparation time: 20 minutes
Baking time: 20 minutes

[6 servings]

TOPPING

1	cup all-purpose flour
1½	teaspoons baking powder
⅛	teaspoon salt
3	tablespoons cold LAND O LAKES® Butter
3	ounces (¾ cup) LAND O LAKES® Cheddar Cheese, shredded
½	cup milk

FILLING

2	cups frozen broccoli cuts, thawed
1½	cups cubed cooked chicken
½	cup chopped carrot
½	cup dried cranberries
½	cup LAND O LAKES® Light Sour Cream
½	cup chicken broth
1	(10¾-ounce) can condensed cream of chicken soup
1	teaspoon dried marjoram leaves
¼	teaspoon pepper
⅛	teaspoon garlic powder

1. Combine flour, baking powder and salt in small bowl; cut in butter until mixture is crumbly. Stir in cheese. Stir in milk just until moistened. Set aside.

2. *Heat oven to 400°.* Stir together all filling ingredients in 3-quart saucepan. Cook over medium heat, stirring occasionally, until mixture just comes to a boil (3 to 5 minutes).

3. Spoon filling into 8-inch square baking dish. Drop topping by tablespoonfuls onto hot chicken mixture. Bake for 20 to 25 minutes or until topping is golden brown.

Nutrition Facts (1 serving): Calories 400; Protein 21 g; Carbohydrate 39 g; Dietary Fiber 4 g; Fat 18 g; Cholesterol 70 mg; Sodium 860 mg

Taco Macaroni Skillet

Enjoy the flavor of tacos in this easy-to-make macaroni skillet supper.

Preparation time: 5 minutes
Cooking time: 24 minutes

[6 servings]

1	pound ground beef
2	teaspoons taco seasoning mix
2	cups water
6	ounces (1½ cups) uncooked dried elbow macaroni
1	(10-ounce) can diced tomatoes with green chilies*
½	cup LAND O LAKES® Sour Cream
4	ounces (1 cup) LAND O LAKES® Cheddar Cheese, shredded

1. Cook ground beef in 10- or 12-inch skillet over medium-high heat, stirring occasionally, until lightly browned (5 to 7 minutes). Drain off fat.

2. Stir in seasoning mix. Add water, uncooked macaroni and tomatoes; mix well. Continue cooking until mixture comes to a full boil (3 to 5 minutes).

3. Reduce heat to low. Cover; cook, stirring occasionally, until macaroni is tender (14 to 16 minutes). Stir in sour cream; sprinkle with cheese. Cover; let stand about 5 minutes before serving.

Nutrition Facts (1 serving): Calories 370; Protein 23 g; Carbohydrate 25 g; Dietary Fiber 2 g; Fat 19 g; Cholesterol 75 mg; Sodium 440 mg

*Substitute 1¼ cups canned diced tomatoes and 2 tablespoons canned chopped green chilies.

Simple Shepherd's Pie

This meat-and-potato pie is a comfort food classic (pictured on cover).

Preparation time: 20 minutes
Baking time: 35 minutes

[6 servings]

1	refrigerated pie crust
1	pound lean ground beef
1	medium (½ cup) onion, chopped
2	cups frozen mixed vegetables (beans, carrots, corn and peas)
1	(10¾-ounce) can condensed cream of celery soup
1½	teaspoons chopped fresh thyme leaves*
3	cups mashed potatoes

1. Heat oven to 375°. Place pie crust in 9-inch pie pan. Crimp or flute edge. Set aside.

2. Cook ground beef and onion in 10-inch skillet over medium heat, stirring occasionally, until beef is browned (9 to 11 minutes). Drain off fat. Stir in vegetables, soup and thyme leaves; continue cooking until heated through (3 to 5 minutes).

3. Spoon meat mixture into pie crust. Spoon mashed potatoes over meat mixture. Bake for 35 to 45 minutes or until potatoes are lightly browned and pie is heated through.

Nutrition Facts (1 serving): Calories 480; Protein 27 g; Carbohydrate 37 g; Dietary Fiber 5 g; Fat 24 g; Cholesterol 75 mg; Sodium 770 mg

*Substitute ½ teaspoon dried thyme leaves.

[kitchen notes]

The original concept of Shepherd's Pie—cooked meat and vegetables in gravy topped with mashed potatoes and then baked—came about when home cooks wanted to make use of the leftover roast from Sunday dinner. This modern variation is easy and can be made even if you don't have leftovers.

Beef Burgundy & Mushrooms

Serve this beef and mushroom main dish with crusty bread and a spinach salad.

Preparation time: 10 minutes
Cooking time: 17 minutes

[6 servings]

2 tablespoons LAND O LAKES® Butter
1 pound beef sirloin *or* round steak, cut into thin strips
1 cup dry red wine *or* beef broth
2 tablespoons all-purpose flour
1 teaspoon finely chopped fresh garlic
½ teaspoon salt
½ teaspoon coarsely ground pepper
¼ teaspoon dry mustard
2 (8-ounce) packages fresh mushrooms, halved
1 medium green pepper, cut into ½-inch pieces
½ medium red onion, thinly sliced, separated into rings

   Hot cooked noodles *or* rice

1. Melt butter in Dutch oven until sizzling; add sirloin strips. Cook over medium-high heat, stirring occasionally, until browned (6 to 8 minutes).

2. Meanwhile, stir together wine, flour, garlic, salt, pepper and dry mustard with wire whisk in small bowl. Add to meat; continue cooking until smooth and bubbly (30 seconds).

3. Add all remaining ingredients *except* noodles. Continue cooking, stirring occasionally, until beef is fork-tender (10 to 12 minutes). Serve over hot cooked noodles.

Nutrition Facts (1 serving without noodles): Calories 180; Protein 17 g; Carbohydrate 8 g; Dietary Fiber 1 g; Fat 8 g; Cholesterol 55 mg; Sodium 250 mg

Fusilli & Bean Bake

This robust pasta-and-bean bake goes well with hearty wheat bread and melon slices.

Preparation time: 20 minutes
Baking time: 35 minutes

[6 servings]

6 ounces (2 cups) uncooked dried multi-colored fusilli (thin corkscrew *or* pasta twists)
6 thick bacon slices, cut into ½-inch pieces
1 medium (½ cup) onion, chopped
½ teaspoon finely chopped fresh garlic
1 (15½-ounce) can cannellini beans, rinsed, drained
1 (15-ounce) can red beans, rinsed, drained
1 (15-ounce) can black-eyed peas, rinsed, drained
1 (14- to 16-ounce) can whole tomatoes, cut up
1 tablespoon chopped fresh oregano leaves*

¼ teaspoon salt
¼ teaspoon pepper
4 ounces (1 cup) LAND O LAKES® Cheddar Cheese, shredded

1. Cook fusilli according to package directions. Drain. Set aside.

2. Cook bacon in 10-inch skillet over medium-high heat until softened (3 to 4 minutes). Stir in onion and garlic. Continue cooking, stirring occasionally, until onion is softened and bacon is crisp (8 to 10 minutes). Drain off fat.

3. Meanwhile, *heat oven to 350°.* Stir together cooked fusilli and all remaining ingredients *except* cheese in 3-quart casserole. Stir in cooked bacon mixture.

4. Cover; bake for 20 minutes. Stir; top with cheese. Continue baking for 15 to 20 minutes or until heated through.

Nutrition Facts (1 serving): Calories 410; Protein 21 g; Carbohydrate 57 g; Dietary Fiber 12 g; Fat 11 g; Cholesterol 25 mg; Sodium 820 mg

*Substitute 1 teaspoon dried oregano leaves.

TIP To make this a meatless dish, omit bacon. Cook vegetables in 2 tablespoons LAND O LAKES® Butter. Continue as directed above.

Beef Burgundy & Mushrooms

Corned Beef Hash

American cheese, hash browns and peppers comprise this extra-easy skillet supper.

Preparation time: 15 minutes
Cooking time: 14 minutes

[6 servings]

2	tablespoons LAND O LAKES® Butter
½	cup chopped onion
½	cup chopped green pepper
½	cup chopped red pepper
1	(2-pound) package Southern-style frozen hash-brown potatoes
2	tablespoons chopped fresh parsley
2	cups chopped cooked corned beef
½	cup chicken broth
¼	teaspoon salt
¼	teaspoon pepper
4	ounces (1 cup) LAND O LAKES® American Cheese, shredded

1. Melt butter in 10-inch skillet until sizzling; add onion and peppers. Cook over medium heat until onion is softened (3 to 4 minutes). Add potatoes and parsley. Continue cooking until potatoes are browned and crispy (8 to 10 minutes).

2. Reduce heat to medium. Stir in corned beef, chicken broth, salt and pepper. Cook until mixture is heated through (3 to 4 minutes).

3. Just before serving, sprinkle with cheese.

Nutrition Facts (1 serving): Calories 520; Protein 31 g; Carbohydrate 44 g; Dietary Fiber 5 g; Fat 26 g; Cholesterol 105 mg; Sodium 1480 mg

Stuffed Chilies with Yellow Rice

Rice and cheese-filled chilies are a colorful south of the border entree.

Preparation time: 30 minutes
Grilling time: 8 minutes

[4 servings]

¾	cup uncooked rice
⅛	teaspoon ground turmeric
8	Anaheim chile peppers
¾	cup chopped Roma tomatoes
¼	cup chopped green onion
2	ounces (½ cup) LAND O LAKES® Monterey Jack Cheese, finely shredded
½	teaspoon salt
	Fresh cilantro leaves, if desired

1. Heat gas grill to medium *or* charcoal grill until coals are ash white.

2. Cook rice with turmeric according to package directions. Drain.

3. Meanwhile, leaving stems intact, cut a slit lengthwise ½ inch from stem to tip of each pepper. Carefully remove seeds and membranes.

4. Combine cooked rice, tomatoes, green onions and cheese in large bowl; mix well. Spoon about *½ cup* rice mixture into each pepper.

5. Place peppers on grill. Cover; grill until peppers are heated through and cheese is melted (8 to 10 minutes). Garnish with cilantro, if desired.

Nutrition Facts (1 serving): Calories 270; Protein 9 g; Carbohydrate 48 g; Dietary Fiber 3 g; Fat 5 g; Cholesterol 15 mg; Sodium 350 mg

TIP Chile peppers' "heat" can cause a burning sensation on tender skin. Be especially careful not to rub your eyes while handling peppers. When chopping peppers, you may want to wear gloves.

Named for opera singer Luisa Tetrazzini, this rich baked dish features noodles and chicken enrobed in a cream sauce flavored with sherry and Parmesan cheese.

Chicken & Red Pepper Tetrazzini

Select convenience foods let you prepare this exquisitely rich dish in less than 30 minutes.

Preparation time: 10 minutes
Cooking time: 19 minutes

[6 (1⅓-cup) servings]

2   tablespoons LAND O LAKES® Butter
1   (15-ounce) package chicken tenders
1   medium (1 cup) red pepper, sliced
2   teaspoons finely chopped fresh garlic
2   (14½-ounce) cans (3½ cups) chicken broth
1   (10¾-ounce) can condensed cream of chicken soup
8   ounces uncooked dried vermicelli (extra thin spaghetti), broken in half
8   ounces fresh mushrooms, sliced
2   tablespoons chopped fresh thyme leaves*
4   ounces (1 cup) grated Parmesan cheese

1. Melt butter in 12-inch skillet until sizzling; add chicken tenders, red pepper and garlic. Cook over medium heat, stirring occasionally, until chicken is no longer pink (7 to 8 minutes). Remove from pan; keep warm.

2. Place broth, soup, vermicelli and mushrooms in same skillet. Cook over medium heat, stirring occasionally, until vermicelli is tender (10 to 12 minutes).

3. Return chicken and peppers to skillet. Stir in thyme. Cook, stirring occasionally, until heated through (2 to 3 minutes).

4. Remove from heat; stir in cheese.

Nutrition Facts (1 serving): Calories 430; Protein 35 g; Carbohydrate 36 g; Dietary Fiber 2 g; Fat 15 g; Cholesterol 70 mg; Sodium 1310 mg

*Substitute 2 teaspoons dried thyme leaves.

TIP Turkey is equally good in this dish, which makes perfect use of Thanksgiving-day leftovers.

New England Chicken & Corn Quiche

Hearty with chicken and corn, this quiche is perfect for a casual supper or winter brunch.

Preparation time: 20 minutes
Baking time: 40 minutes

[8 servings]

PASTRY

1   9-inch unbaked pie pastry

FILLING

4   eggs
1½ cups milk
¾   cup cubed cooked chicken
½   cup whole kernel corn
¼   cup chopped roasted red peppers
4   ounces (1 cup) LAND O LAKES® Cheddar Cheese, shredded
2   tablespoons sliced green onions
1   tablespoon all-purpose flour
1   tablespoon chopped fresh basil leaves
½   teaspoon salt
¼   teaspoon pepper

1. Heat oven to 400°. Line 9-inch pie plate with pastry.

2. Beat eggs slightly in large bowl; stir in milk. Stir in all remaining filling ingredients; mix well.

3. Pour into crust. Bake for 40 to 45 minutes or until knife inserted near center comes out clean. Let stand 10 minutes.

4. To serve, cut into wedges.

Nutrition Facts (1 serving): Calories 340; Protein 14 g; Carbohydrate 22 g; Dietary Fiber 1 g; Fat 21 g; Cholesterol 135 mg; Sodium 510 mg

TIP To roast red peppers, wash and quarter peppers, removing seeds and ribs. Place skin side up on baking sheet or broiler pan and broil approximately 4 inches below heat until skin is blackened and charred. Remove from oven and place blackened peppers in a bag or shallow covered dish to steam; after 15 minutes, slip off skins.

Creamy Pasta Parmesan

Enjoy the rich and creamy taste of Alfredo without the guilt in this lower-fat version of a comfort food favorite.

Preparation time: 15 minutes
Cooking time: 2 minutes

[4 servings]

8   ounces uncooked dried fettuccine
½   cup LAND O LAKES® Light Sour Cream
½   cup fat free milk
1   cup frozen green peas
⅔   cup freshly shredded Parmesan cheese
¼   cup finely chopped green onions
    Cracked black pepper, if desired

1. Cook fettuccine according to package directions. Drain.

2. Meanwhile, combine sour cream and milk in small bowl with wire whisk; mix well.

3. Combine cooked fettuccine, sour cream mixture, peas, ½ cup cheese and green onions in same pan. Cook over medium heat, tossing gently, until thoroughly heated (2 to 3 minutes).

4. To serve, spoon fettuccine mixture onto platter; top with remaining cheese and black pepper. Serve immediately.

Nutrition Facts (1 serving): Calories 360; Protein 19 g; Carbohydrate 53 g; Dietary Fiber 3 g; Fat 8 g; Cholesterol 20 mg; Sodium 400 mg

TIP If you prefer pasta with a thinner consistency, add 2 to 3 tablespoons milk.

New England Chicken & Corn Quiche

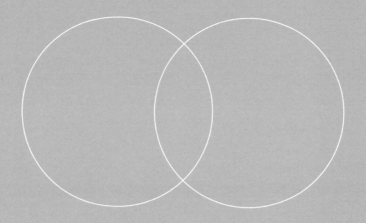

Salads and Sides

Once relegated to a quiet corner of the table, salads and side dishes are attaining comfort food status in their own right. In this chapter, old favorites like Garlic Mashed Potatoes and Three Bean Salad share center plate with new traditions such as Butter-Roasted Vegetables and Overnight Oriental Salad.

Country-Style Spoon Bread

Technique

Always choose the freshest vegetables available. Trust your senses, and avoid wilted, bruised or limp vegetables in favor of those with firm texture and bright, even color. If the fresh vegetables available on a given day are not top quality, you are better off working with good quality frozen vegetables.

Purchasing vegetables that have already been cleaned, chopped or shredded saves preparation time. Sliced or shredded potatoes are available in the dairy case.

Unlike many vegetable side dishes, most of these may be made ahead for easy entertaining. Some even taste better if they've had a chance for the spices to marry, Overnight Oriental Salad and Three Bean Salad among them. Others, such as Cheesy Baked Carrots, Twice Baked Potatoes and Green Bean Almond Bake, may be assembled in advance.

Country-Style Spoon Bread

Old-fashioned spoon bread with honey butter makes a tasty brunch offering or partner to a main dish.

Preparation time: 20 minutes
Baking time: 40 minutes

[8 servings]

SPOON BREAD
3   cups milk
1   cup yellow cornmeal
2   tablespoons LAND O LAKES® Butter, softened
1   teaspoon baking powder
½   teaspoon salt
3   eggs, separated

HONEY BUTTER
½   cup LAND O LAKES® Butter, softened
2   tablespoons honey

1. Heat oven to 350°. Combine *2 cups* milk and cornmeal in 2-quart saucepan. Cook over medium heat, stirring constantly, until all milk is absorbed and mixture is thickened (5 to 7 minutes). Remove from heat.

2. Add 2 tablespoons butter, baking powder and salt; stir until well mixed and butter is melted. Beat in remaining milk and egg yolks with wire whisk until smooth. Transfer to large bowl; set aside.

3. Beat egg whites in small mixer bowl at high speed, scraping bowl often, until stiff peaks form (1 to 2 minutes). Gently stir into cornmeal mixture until smooth.

4. Gently pour into greased 2-quart casserole. Bake for 40 to 45 minutes or until golden brown and top springs back when touched lightly in center.

5. Meanwhile, stir together all honey butter ingredients in small bowl. Serve with warm spoon bread.

Nutrition Facts (1 serving): Calories 280; Protein 7 g; Carbohydrate 23 g; Dietary Fiber 1 g; Fat 18 g; Cholesterol 125 mg; Sodium 410 mg

TIP Spoon bread is a pudding baked in a casserole dish and so soft it's eaten with a spoon—hence the name. It's most often served as an accompaniment to seasoned meats.

Cheesy Baked Carrots

The perfect Sunday dinner side dish, this casserole pairs well with meatloaf or porkchops.

Preparation time: 25 minutes
Baking time: 30 minutes

[8 (½-cup) servings]

CARROTS

4   medium (4 cups) carrots, sliced ¼-inch, cooked
2   tablespoons LAND O LAKES® Butter
¼   cup finely chopped parsley
1   tablespoon finely chopped onion
2   tablespoons all-purpose flour
½   teaspoon salt
¼   teaspoon dry mustard
⅛   teaspoon pepper
1   cup milk
4   ounces (1 cup) LAND O LAKES® American Cheese, cubed

TOPPING

3   cups dry bread cubes
¼   cup LAND O LAKES® Butter, melted

1. Heat oven to 350°. Place carrots in 1½-quart casserole. Set aside.

2. Melt 2 tablespoons butter in 2-quart saucepan until sizzling; add celery and onion. Cook over medium heat, stirring occasionally, until crisply tender (3 to 4 minutes). Stir in flour, salt, dry mustard and pepper. Continue cooking until smooth and bubbly (1 minute). Gradually stir in milk with wire whisk. Continue cooking, stirring occasionally, until mixture thickens and comes to a full boil (4 to 5 minutes). Boil 1 minute.

3. Remove saucepan from heat. Stir in cheese until melted. Pour sauce over carrots.

4. Stir together bread cubes and ¼ cup butter in medium bowl; sprinkle over carrots. Bake for 30 to 40 minutes or until bubbly in center and bread cubes are lightly browned.

Nutrition Facts (1 serving): Calories 210; Protein 6 g; Carbohydrate 15 g; Dietary Fiber 2 g; Fat 15 g; Cholesterol 40 mg; Sodium 530 mg

[kitchen notes]

While technically a late fall and winter vegetable, carrots are available
all year in most places. They are an excellent source of vitamin A,
and will retain their flavor and texture for several days when stored, unrinsed,
in plastic bags in the crisper drawer of your refrigerator.

Three-Bean Salad

A crisp and colorful bean salad is an ideal accompaniment to a family dinner.

Preparation time: 15 minutes
Chilling time: 2 hours

[6 servings]

DRESSING

⅓	cup herbed vinegar *or* cider vinegar
2	tablespoons sugar
1	tablespoon chopped fresh parsley
2	tablespoons olive *or* vegetable oil
¼	teaspoon pepper

SALAD

1	cup julienne-cut red onion strips
1	cup julienne-cut red pepper strips
1	(15-ounce) can garbanzo beans (chickpeas), rinsed, drained
1	(15-ounce) can dark kidney beans, rinsed, drained
1	(15-ounce) can pinto beans, rinsed, drained
1	(10-ounce) jar (1 cup) pepperoncini, drained, seeded, sliced

1. Stir together all dressing ingredients in small bowl. Set aside.

2. Combine all salad ingredients in large bowl. Add dressing; toss to coat. Cover; refrigerate, stirring every hour, at least 2 hours.

Nutrition Facts (1 serving): Calories 280; Protein 11 g; Carbohydrate 46 g; Dietary Fiber 10 g; Fat 6 g; Cholesterol 0 mg; Sodium 660 mg

TIP Be creative and vary the beans in this salad to suit your mood, or the season. Navy beans and black or turtle beans provide contrast to pintos and kidney beans; green beans and wax beans add new texture and dimension; fresh baby limas signal the start of summer.

TIP Pepperocini are pickled Italian peppers. They are available in the condiment section of large supermarkets.

Rainbow Rice

Colorful bell peppers and Roma tomatoes flavor this easily prepared side dish.

Preparation time: 15 minutes
Cooking time: 24 minutes

[6 servings]

1	tablespoon LAND O LAKES® Butter
¼	cup finely chopped onion
2	teaspoons finely chopped fresh garlic
½	cup frozen whole kernel corn
½	cup chopped orange, red *and/or* yellow pepper
1	(14½-ounce) can chicken broth
½	teaspoon salt
1	cup long grain white rice
½	cup frozen peas
2	Roma tomatoes, chopped

1. Melt butter in 2-quart saucepan until sizzling; add onion and garlic. Cook over medium heat, stirring constantly, until onion is softened (1 to 2 minutes). Add corn and pepper. Continue cooking, stirring occasionally, until peppers are crisply tender (2 to 3 minutes).

2. Add chicken broth and salt. Continue cooking until mixture comes to a boil (3 to 5 minutes). Reduce heat to low. Add rice. Cover; cook 15 minutes. Stir in peas and tomatoes. Cover; continue cooking until rice is tender (5 to 8 minutes). Remove from heat; let stand 5 minutes or until all liquid is absorbed.

Nutrition Facts (1 serving): Calories 170; Protein 5 g; Carbohydrate 32 g; Dietary Fiber 2 g; Fat 2.5 g; Cholesterol 5 mg; Sodium 430 mg

Three-Bean Salad

Light Pasta Salad Italiano

This light-yet-hearty pasta salad is a great make-ahead dish.

Preparation time: 25 minutes
Chilling time: 2 hours

[6 servings]

4	ounces (1¼ cups) uncooked dried tri-colored rotini (corkscrew *or* pasta twists)
½	cup reduced-calorie creamy Italian dressing
8	ounces (2 cups) LAND O LAKES® Mozzarella Cheese, cubed ½-inch
12	cherry tomatoes, halved
1	medium green pepper, cubed ½-inch

1. Cook rotini according to package directions. Rinse with cold water; drain

2. Combine all ingredients in large bowl; toss until well coated. Cover; refrigerate at least 2 hours.

Nutrition Facts (1 serving): Calories 200; Protein 13 g; Carbohydrate 18 g; Dietary Fiber 1 g; Fat 9 g; Cholesterol 20 mg; Sodium 360 mg

Garlic Mashed Potatoes

Roasted garlic adds gourmet flavor to this irresistible side dish.

Preparation time: 15 minutes
Cooking time: 24 minutes

[6 (¾-cup) servings]

5	medium-size potatoes, peeled, cut into eighths
1	teaspoon salt
½	cup warm milk
6	tablespoons LAND O LAKES® Butter, softened
1	teaspoon purchased prepared roasted garlic
	Salt
	Pepper

1. Place potatoes in 4-quart saucepan or Dutch oven. Add enough water to cover; add 1 teaspoon salt. Bring to a boil over high heat (7 to 9 minutes). Reduce heat to medium. Cook until potatoes are fork tender (15 to 18 minutes). Drain.

2. Place potatoes in large mixer bowl. Add milk, butter and garlic. Beat at medium speed until smooth (2 to 3 minutes). Season with salt and pepper.

TIP *Roasting your own garlic is fun and easy to do:* Heat oven to 350°. Cut ¼ to ½ inch from top of garlic bulb to expose cloves. Remove most of outer skin from bulb, leaving bulb intact and cloves unpeeled. Place bulb, cut-side up, on 8-inch piece aluminum foil. Drizzle with 1 teaspoon olive oil; sprinkle lightly with salt and pepper. Wrap in foil. Bake for 45 to 55 minutes or until softened. Cool slightly. Separate the cloves and press cloves slightly to squeeze out softened garlic. Use roasted garlic in recipes or spread on French bread. (Makes about 3 tablespoons)

Nutrition Facts (1 serving): Calories 190; Protein 3 g; Carbohydrate 18 g; Dietary Fiber 2 g; Fat 12 g; Cholesterol 35 mg; Sodium 490 mg

Salad days are any days where a mixed dish of good things tops the menu— be they greens, beans, or heartier fare.

Overnight Oriental Salad

Tote this delicious make-ahead salad to a spring or summer gathering.

Preparation time: 25 minutes
Chilling time: 4 hours

[10 (¾-cup) servings]

6	cups thinly sliced Chinese cabbage
1	cup fresh bean sprouts
1	(8-ounce) can water chestnuts, drained, sliced
2	cups broken fresh pea pods, tips and strings removed
1	cup coarsely chopped red onion
1	(8-ounce) can crushed pineapple
1	(9-ounce) package frozen cooked chicken breast pieces, thawed*
1	(3-ounce) package chicken-flavored ramen noodle soup mix
½	cup LAND O LAKES® Sour Cream
½	cup mayonnaise
3	tablespoons rice vinegar**

1. Layer cabbage, sprouts, water chestnuts, pea pods and onion in large salad bowl. Spoon pineapple with juice over mixture. Add chicken pieces. Stir together seasoning packet from soup mix, sour cream, mayonnaise and vinegar. Spoon over salad, spreading to cover. Cover tightly; refrigerate 4 hours.

2. To serve, toss salad. Break ramen noodles into small pieces. Add to salad; toss lightly to coat.

Nutrition Facts (1 serving): Calories 240; Protein 11 g; Carbohydrate 19 g; Dietary Fiber 3 g; Fat 15 g; Cholesterol 35 mg; Sodium 270 mg

*Substitute 2 cups leftover cooked chicken *or* turkey.

**Substitute white wine vinegar *or* a combination of 1 tablespoon cider vinegar and 1 tablespoon apple juice.

TIP Chicken can be omitted for a delicious salad to serve as an accompaniment to meat or poultry.

Fruit Salad with Sweet Orange Cream

A hint of curry lends unexpected savor to this creamy fruit dish.

Preparation time: 15 minutes

[6 servings]

DRESSING

½	cup LAND O LAKES® Light Sour Cream
¼	cup frozen orange juice concentrate, thawed
3	tablespoons fat free milk
2	teaspoons honey
¼-½	teaspoon curry powder

SALAD

1	cup strawberry halves
1	cup red apple slices
1	cup seedless green grapes
1	(11-ounce) can mandarin orange segments, well-drained*
8	cups mixed salad greens

1. Combine all dressing ingredients in small bowl with wire whisk; mix well.

2. Combine fruit in large bowl.

3. To serve, divide greens among six salad plates; top with fruit and dressing.

Nutrition Facts (1 serving): Calories 120; Protein 3 g; Carbohydrate 26 g; Dietary Fiber 3 g; Fat 2 g; Cholesterol 5 mg; Sodium 45 mg

*Substitute 2 cups canned pineapple chunks in juice, well-drained.

Classic Waldorf Salad

Coarsely chopped dates add depth to this fresh, all-season salad.

Preparation time: 20 minutes
Chilling time: 1 hour

[8 (½-cup) servings]

¼	cup mayonnaise
¼	cup LAND O LAKES® Sour Cream
1	tablespoon sugar
1	teaspoon lemon juice
1	cup sliced celery
½	cup coarsely chopped walnuts, toasted
½	cup chopped dates
2	medium (2 cups) red *and/or* green apples, cubed ½-inch

1. Stir together mayonnaise, sour cream, sugar and lemon juice in large bowl. Add all remaining ingredients; toss lightly to coat. Cover; refrigerate at least 1 hour.

Nutrition Facts (1 serving): Calories 170; Protein 2 g; Carbohydrate 18 g; Dietary Fiber 2 g; Fat 12 g; Cholesterol 10 mg; Sodium 55 mg

TIP Created at New York's Waldorf-Astoria Hotel in the 1890s, the original version of this salad contained only apples, celery and mayonnaise. Chopped walnuts became an integral part of the recipe later.

Fruit Salad with Sweet Orange Cream

Slow-Cooked Country Baked Beans

Long, slow cooking brings out old-time flavor in these hearty baked beans.

Preparation time: 15 minutes
Standing time: 8 hours
Cooking time: 5 hours

[10 (1¼-cup) servings]

2	cups dried great Northern beans
1	cup dried kidney beans
2½	cups hot water
1	cup firmly packed brown sugar
½	cup dark molasses
¼	cup country-style Dijon mustard
2	medium (1½ cups) onions, chopped
4	slices thick sliced bacon, cut into 1-inch pieces

1. Combine great Northern beans, kidney beans and enough cold water to cover in Dutch oven. Let stand 8 hours or overnight. Drain.

2. Combine beans, hot water and all remaining ingredients in electric slow cooker. Cook on High for 5 to 6 hours, or on Low for 10 to 12 hours or until beans are tender and sauce is thickened.

Nutrition Facts (1 serving): Calories 400; Protein 14 g; Carbohydrate 69 g; Dietary Fiber 8 g; Fat 9 g; Cholesterol 10 mg; Sodium 280 mg

TIP For same day preparation do not soak beans overnight. Instead, cook great Northern beans, kidney beans and water in Dutch oven over high heat until water comes to a full boil. Reduce heat to medium. Cook 2 minutes. Remove from heat. Cover; let stand 1 hour. Continue as directed above.

Skillet German Potato Salad

Rich with the flavors of bacon and chives, this easy side is ready in no time.

Preparation time: 15 minutes
Cooking time: 11 minutes

[8 (¾-cup) servings]

6	slices bacon, cut into ½-inch pieces
½	cup sliced ¼-inch celery
1	(24-ounce) package frozen country-style seasoned potato chunks
1	medium (½ cup) onion, coarsely chopped
½	cup beef broth
¼	cup firmly packed brown sugar
1	tablespoon all-purpose flour
⅛	teaspoon coarsely ground black pepper
⅓	cup chopped fresh chives *or* green onions

1. Cook bacon in 12-inch nonstick skillet over medium heat, stirring occasionally, until crisp (3 to 5 minutes). Remove bacon; set aside. *Reserve bacon drippings in skillet.*

2. Add celery, potatoes and onion to reserved bacon drippings. Cook over medium heat, stirring occasionally, until potatoes are browned and onion is softened (7 to 10 minutes).

3. Meanwhile, stir together beef broth, brown sugar, flour and pepper in small bowl. Pour over potatoes in skillet. Continue cooking, stirring constantly, until mixture thickens and comes to a boil (1 to 2 minutes).

4. Stir in bacon and chives.

Nutrition Facts (1 serving): Calories 200; Protein 4 g; Carbohydrate 24 g; Dietary Fiber 2 g; Fat 10 g; Cholesterol 10 mg; Sodium 210 mg

TIP This bacon-studded potato salad may be served hot or at room temperature. Paired with a crisp green salad, good bread and cheese, it makes a fine, light supper.

Sweet Potatoes with Sugared Pecans

Rich, crunchy pecans enhance this sweet potato side dish.

Preparation time: 15 minutes
Cooking time: 35 minutes
Baking time: 20 minutes

[6 servings]

POTATOES

4 medium-size sweet potatoes *or* yams, cut into 2-inch chunks
2 tablespoons LAND O LAKES® Butter
1 tablespoon firmly packed brown sugar
1 teaspoon ground cinnamon
½ teaspoon salt
⅛ teaspoon pepper

PECANS

1 tablespoon LAND O LAKES® Butter
¼ cup chopped pecans
2 teaspoons sugar

¼ cup sliced green onions

1. Combine sweet potatoes and enough water to cover in 4-quart saucepan. Cook over high heat until water comes to a boil (5 to 6 minutes). Reduce heat to medium-high. Cook until potatoes are tender (30 to 35 minutes). Drain. Cool slightly. Peel potatoes.

2. *Heat oven to 375°.* Place sweet potatoes and all remaining potato ingredients in large mixer bowl. Beat at medium speed, scraping bowl often, until smooth (1 to 2 minutes).

3. Spoon potato mixture into lightly greased 2-quart casserole. Cover; bake for 20 to 25 minutes or until heated through.

4. Meanwhile, melt 1 tablespoon butter in small nonstick skillet until sizzling; add pecans and sugar. Cook over medium-low heat, stirring constantly, until pecans are golden (2 to 3 minutes). Remove from heat.

5. Just before serving, sprinkle potatoes with pecans and green onions.

Nutrition Facts (1 serving): Calories 180; Protein 2 g; Carbohydrate 24 g; Dietary Fiber 3 g; Fat 9 g; Cholesterol 15 mg; Sodium 250 mg

[kitchen notes]

While many use the words "yam" and "sweet potato" interchangeably, the two are, in fact, very different. In botanical terms, a yam is a tuber and a sweet potato is a root. The most common types of yams are native to the tropics and simply wouldn't thrive in American soil. Yams have a white interior and are typically longer than sweet potatoes, which have an orangey-brown flesh and are much smaller.

Blue Cheese & Pepper Salad

Mixed greens and tender summer vegetables are enlivened with a blue cheese and sour cream dressing.

Preparation time: 20 minutes

[4 servings]

DRESSING
½   cup LAND O LAKES® Fat Free Sour Cream
¼   cup fat free milk
2   teaspoons finely chopped fresh garlic
½   teaspoon salt

SALAD
1   (10-ounce) bag (6 cups) mixed salad greens
16 cherry tomatoes
8   (½-inch) peeled cucumber slices, quartered
1   cup frozen green peas, cooked, drained
½   cup red onion rings, separated
2   ounces (½ cup) crumbled blue cheese
    Freshly ground black pepper

1. Combine sour cream, milk, garlic and salt in small bowl with wire whisk; mix well. Cover; refrigerate until serving time.

2. To serve, divide greens among four plates. Top each with tomatoes, cucumbers, peas and onions; sprinkle with blue cheese. Drizzle each serving with *3 tablespoons* dressing; sprinkle with pepper.

Nutrition Facts (1 serving): Calories 150; Protein 9 g; Carbohydrate 19 g; Dietary Fiber 4 g; Fat 5 g; Cholesterol 15 mg; Sodium 580 mg

Green Bean Almond Bake

A roasted red pepper-studded cream sauce enhances crisply tender green beans.

Preparation time: 15 minutes
Baking time: 40 minutes

[6 (⅔-cup) servings]

BEANS
1   (16-ounce) package frozen cut green beans
3   tablespoons LAND O LAKES® Butter
3   tablespoons all-purpose flour
1   teaspoon instant chicken bouillon granules
1¼ cups milk
½   cup chopped onion
¼   cup chopped roasted red peppers

TOPPING
½   cup sliced almonds
¼   cup dry bread crumbs
1   tablespoon LAND O LAKES® Butter, melted

1. Heat oven to 350°. Microwave beans in 1½-quart baking dish according to package directions. Drain.

2. Meanwhile, melt butter in 2-quart saucepan until sizzling; stir in flour and bouillon granules. Cook over medium heat until smooth and bubbly (1 minute). Gradually stir in milk with wire whisk. Continue cooking, stirring occasionally, until mixture thickens and comes to a full boil (4 to 5 minutes). Boil 1 minute.

3. Remove from heat; stir in onion and roasted red peppers. Add mixture to cooked beans.

4. Combine all topping ingredients in small bowl; sprinkle over bean mixture. Bake for 40 to 45 minutes or until heated through.

Nutrition Facts (1 serving): Calories 200; Protein 6 g; Carbohydrate 16 g; Dietary Fiber 4 g; Fat 13 g; Cholesterol 25 mg; Sodium 260 mg

Blue Cheese & Pepper Salad

Mixed Green Salad with Orange Raspberry Dressing

Garnish this tasty green salad with fresh raspberries and toasted almond slices.

Preparation time: 20 minutes

[6 servings]

SALAD

6	cups mixed fancy salad greens
½	cup chopped red onion
1	(11-ounce) can mandarin orange segments, drained

DRESSING

⅓	cup frozen orange juice concentrate
¼	cup water
3	tablespoons raspberry vinegar
1	tablespoon vegetable oil
¼	teaspoon salt

GARNISH

1	cup fresh raspberries
¼	cup sliced almonds, toasted

1. Gently toss together all salad ingredients in large bowl.

2. Combine all dressing ingredients in small bowl. Pour *⅓ cup* dressing over salad; toss gently to coat. Sprinkle with raspberries and almonds. Serve with remaining dressing.

Nutrition Facts (1 serving): Calories 110; Protein 3 g; Carbohydrate 16 g; Dietary Fiber 4 g; Fat 5 g; Cholesterol 0 mg; Sodium 110 mg

TIP To toast almonds, heat oven to 350°. Place almonds in pie pan. Bake for 5 to 10 minutes, stirring occasionally, or until golden brown.

Potato Salad with Mustard Mayonnaise

This creamy potato salad features accents of mustard seed and refreshing cucumber.

Preparation time: 30 minutes
Chilling time: 2 hours

[8 servings]

4	cups water
1	teaspoon salt
4	cups quartered small new red potatoes
½	cup celery, sliced ¼-inch
½	cup mayonnaise
¼	cup chopped red onion
2	hard-cooked eggs, chopped
1	tablespoon mustard seed
2	tablespoons country-style Dijon mustard
½	teaspoon salt
½	teaspoon coarsely ground pepper
⅓	cup chopped fresh parsley
1	medium (1 cup) cucumber, sliced ⅛-inch, cut in half

1. Combine water and 1 teaspoon salt in 3-quart saucepan. Cook over high heat until water comes to a full boil (7 to 9 minutes). Add potatoes. Continue cooking until potatoes are fork-tender (12 to 15 minutes). Drain. Rinse with cold water.

2. Stir together all remaining ingredients *except* parsley and cucumber in large bowl. Add potatoes, parsley and cucumber; toss to coat. Cover; refrigerate at least 2 hours to blend flavors.

Nutrition Facts (1 serving): Calories 200; Protein 4 g; Carbohydrate 16 g; Dietary Fiber 1 g; Fat 13 g; Cholesterol 75 mg; Sodium 350 mg

Many of these recipes may be combined for light yet satisfying main dish fare. Choose two or three dishes whose flavors complement each other, and serve with bread and cheese for a wholesome meal.

Twice-Baked Potatoes

These hearty and flavorful twice-baked potatoes are enriched with sour cream.

Preparation time: 10 minutes
Baking time: 75 minutes
Cooling time: 15 minutes

[8 servings]

4   large baking potatoes
½   cup LAND O LAKES® Sour Cream
¼   cup LAND O LAKES® Butter, softened
1   tablespoon chopped fresh chives
½   teaspoon salt
⅛   teaspoon pepper

      Chopped fresh chives, if desired
      Paprika, if desired

1. Heat oven to 400°. Prick potatoes with fork to allow steam to escape. Bake for 60 to 75 minutes or until fork-tender. *Reduce oven temperature to 375°.*

2. Cut potatoes in half lengthwise. Let cool about 15 minutes. Scoop out potatoes, using spoon, leaving ½-inch shell. Set aside shells.

3. Combine scooped-out potato, sour cream, butter, 1 tablespoon chives, salt and pepper in large mixer bowl. Beat at medium speed, scraping bowl often, until smooth (1 to 2 minutes).

4. Fill shells with potato mixture. Place on ungreased baking sheet. Bake for 15 to 20 minutes or until heated through. Sprinkle with chopped chives and paprika, if desired.

Nutrition Facts (1 serving): Calories 180; Protein 3 g; Carbohydrate 24 g; Dietary Fiber 2 g; Fat 9 g; Cholesterol 25 mg; Sodium 210 mg

Butter-Roasted Vegetables

Roasted vegetables seasoned with fresh herbs complement chicken, beef or fish.

Preparation time: 15 minutes
Baking time: 25 minutes

[4 servings]

4   cups any combination fresh vegetables, cut as desired (butternut squash, baby carrots, zucchini, small new red potatoes, onion, garlic cloves, mushrooms, green *or* red peppers, green beans, asparagus)
3   tablespoons LAND O LAKES® Butter, melted
2   teaspoons chopped fresh chives
1   teaspoon chopped fresh oregano leaves
1   teaspoon garlic salt

1. Heat oven to 400°. Combine all vegetables in 13x9-inch baking pan. Add butter, chives, oregano and garlic salt; toss lightly.

2. Bake for 25 to 35 minutes or until vegetables are crisply tender and lightly browned.

Nutrition Facts (1 serving): Calories 130; Protein 2 g; Carbohydrate 12 g; Dietary Fiber 2 g; Fat 9 g; Cholesterol 25 mg; Sodium 510 mg

Two-Bean Caesar Salad

Beans, onion and yellow pepper give this Caesar salad added taste and texture.

Preparation time: 10 minutes

[6 servings]

½   cup chopped red onion
½   cup prepared Caesar salad dressing
1   (15-ounce) can black beans, rinsed, drained
1   (15-ounce) can garbanzo beans (chickpeas), rinsed, drained
1   (2-ounce) jar diced pimientos, drained
1   medium yellow pepper, cut into ½-inch pieces

1   (10-ounce) package Italian blend salad greens
     Freshly grated Parmesan cheese, if desired
     Croutons, if desired

1. Combine onion, salad dressing, beans, pimientos and pepper in medium bowl.

2. To serve, divide greens evenly among six salad plates; top each with about ⅔ *cup* bean mixture. Sprinkle with Parmesan cheese and croutons, if desired.

Nutrition Facts (1 serving): Calories 230; Protein 10 g; Carbohydrate 29 g; Dietary Fiber 9 g; Fat 8 g; Cholesterol 15 mg; Sodium 440 mg

Butter-Roasted Vegetables

Garden Vegetable Pasta Salad

Fresh basil gives this pasta salad a bright new flavor.

Preparation time: 25 minutes
Chilling time: 1 hour

[12 (1/2-cup) servings]

PASTA

6   ounces (2 cups) uncooked rotini (corkscrew *or* pasta twists)

DRESSING

1   (1.05-ounce) package fat free Italian salad dressing mix
²/₃ cup water
¼   cup white wine vinegar
1   tablespoon olive oil

VEGETABLES

2   cups small broccoli florets
¼   cup fresh basil leaves, torn into small pieces
2   medium (1 cup) carrots, sliced
1   medium (½ cup) red onion, chopped
1   medium red *or* yellow pepper, chopped

1. Cook rotini according to package directions. Rinse with cold water; drain.

2. Meanwhile, combine all dressing ingredients in small jar with tight-fitting lid; shake well.

3. Combine rotini, dressing and all vegetable ingredients in large bowl. Cover; refrigerate at least 1 hour. Toss gently before serving.

Nutrition Facts (1 serving): Calories 80; Protein 2 g; Carbohydrate 15 g; Dietary Fiber 1 g; Fat 1 g; Cholesterol 0 mg; Sodium 180 mg

Mediterranean Lemon Pasta Salad

Fresh and sun-dried tomatoes give this salad its sunny flavor.

Preparation time: 30 minutes
Chilling time: 2 hours

[6 (1-cup) servings]

4   ounces uncooked dried rosamarina pasta (orzo)
1   tablespoon LAND O LAKES® Butter
2   cups chopped green, orange, red *and/or* yellow peppers
1   cup chopped onion
2   teaspoons dried Italian seasoning
1½ cups chopped tomatoes
½   cup chopped cucumber
¼   cup finely chopped fresh parsley
¼   cup pitted ripe olives, drained, halved
1   (14-ounce) can quartered artichoke hearts, drained
2   tablespoons lemon juice
½   teaspoon salt

    Belgian endive, if desired

1. Cook pasta according to package directions. Drain. Set aside.

2. Melt butter in Dutch oven until sizzling; add peppers, onion and Italian seasoning. Cook over medium-high heat, stirring occasionally, until peppers are just tender (6 to 8 minutes). Remove from heat.

3. Combine cooked pasta, pepper mixture and all remaining ingredients *except* Belgian endive; toss gently. Cover; refrigerate at least 2 hours to blend flavors.

4. Garnish with Belgian endive and additional parsley, if desired.

Nutrition Facts (1 serving): Calories 160; Protein 6 g; Carbohydrate 28 g; Dietary Fiber 6 g; Fat 3.5 g; Cholesterol 5 mg; Sodium 290 mg

Mediterranean Lemon Pasta Salad

Starters and Snacks

Given life's busy pace, three meals don't always suit the framework of a day—all the more reason what we do eat should nourish body and soul. Filling yet healthful, options like the Focaccia Hero, Chicken Salad Wraps, and Italian Nachos are made to order for families on the go.

Layered Tortilla Pie

Technique

These quick-to-prepare foods make easy light meals or hearty hors d'oeuvres for casual entertaining. Try the Vegetarian Pizza, the Really Deviled Eggs and the Blue Cheese Tomato Tart for starters at a backyard barbecue or to pass on trays at a festive holiday open house.

For flavorful, nutritious snacks at a moment's notice, keep a variety of spreads and condiments on hand— interesting mustards, flavored mayonnaise, canned refried beans, salsas and packages of shredded cheese are staples for the pantry or refrigerator.

Layered Tortilla Pie

This simple main dish takes center stage at game-day gatherings or a Cinco de Mayo party.

Preparation time: 30 minutes
Baking time: 40 minutes

[8 servings]

1	pound ground beef
1	cup chopped onion
2	teaspoons finely chopped fresh garlic
2	tablespoons taco seasoning mix
8	ounces (2 cups) LAND O LAKES® Chedarella® Cheese, shredded
8	(10-inch) flour tortillas
1	(10-ounce) can enchilada sauce
1	(16-ounce) can refried beans
2	tablespoons chopped green chilies
1	(14½-ounce) can diced tomatoes, drained
1	(2¼-ounce) can sliced pitted ripe olives, drained

LAND O LAKES® Sour Cream, if desired
Fresh cilantro, if desired

1. Heat oven to 375°. Spray 12-inch pizza pan with no stick cooking spray. Set aside.

2. Cook ground beef, onion and garlic in 10-inch skillet over medium-high heat, stirring occasionally, until beef is browned (5 to 7 minutes). Drain. Stir in taco seasoning mix; set aside.

3. To assemble pie, place *1 tortilla* on 12-inch pizza pan; spread with about *2½ tablespoons* enchilada sauce. Repeat with second tortilla and sauce. Top with *half* the beef mixture and *1 cup* cheese. Place *1 tortilla* on top; spread with sauce. Top with *1 tortilla* spread with refried beans and chilies. Repeat layers of 2 more tortillas and sauce; top with remaining beef mixture. Place last 2 tortillas and remaining sauce over beef. Top with tomatoes, olives and remaining 1 cup cheese.

4. Bake for 40 to 45 minutes or until heated through. Let stand 10 minutes before cutting into wedges with serrated knife. Garnish with sour cream and cilantro.

Nutrition Facts (1 serving): Calories 530; Protein 27 g; Carbohydrate 51 g; Dietary Fiber 6 g; Fat 24 g; Cholesterol 70 mg; Sodium 1130 mg

TIP If you enjoy Mexican food, keep south-of-the-border staples in your pantry. With tortillas, refried beans, chopped green chilies, ripe olives, enchilada sauce, diced tomatoes, chili powder, cumin, cheese and sour cream on hand, you'll always be ready to indulge your next Mexican food craving.

Quick Veggie & Cheese Quesadillas

For best results, prepare this tasty appetizer once most of your guests have arrived.

Preparation time: 15 minutes
Cooking time: 12 minutes

[24 appetizers]

1½ cups fresh mushrooms, thinly sliced
1 (14½-ounce) can diced tomatoes with roasted garlic, drained
1 (2¼-ounce) can sliced black olives, drained
2 small (1½ cups) zucchini, thinly sliced

6 (10-inch) flour tortillas
3 ounces (¾ cup) LAND O LAKES® Monterey Jack Cheese, shredded
3 tablespoons LAND O LAKES® Butter

LAND O LAKES® Sour Cream

1. Combine mushrooms, tomatoes, olives and zucchini in medium bowl; mix well. Spoon about *¾ cup* mixture on *half* of tortilla; top with *2 tablespoons* cheese. Fold tortilla in half. Repeat with 1 tortilla.

2. Melt *1 tablespoon* butter in 12-inch nonstick skillet until sizzling. Spread butter to coat bottom of skillet. Place 2 folded tortillas in skillet. Cook over medium heat until bottom of tortilla is lightly browned (2 to 4 minutes). Turn; continue cooking until browned (2 to 4 minutes).

3. Remove tortillas from skillet; cut each tortilla into 4 wedges. Dollop with sour cream. Repeat with remaining tortillas and butter.

Nutrition Facts (1 appetizer): Calories 80; Protein 2 g; Carbohydrate 9 g; Dietary Fiber 1 g; Fat 4 g; Cholesterol 5 mg; Sodium 200 mg

[kitchen notes]

Quesadillas are a Mexican specialty easily prepared at home.
Made using flour tortillas that are folded in half and filled with ingredients
like cheese, refried beans and cooked meat, quesadillas are baked,
cut into wedges and served with cooling sides of
salsa, guacamole and sour cream.

Focaccia Hero

*Vary the flavor of this hearty
sandwich by using different
salad dressings.*

Preparation time: 10 minutes

[8 servings]

1   (1-pound) round focaccia
    bread*
1/2 cup creamy Italian salad
    dressing
12 lettuce leaves
4   ounces thinly sliced deli hard
    salami
10 (3/4 ounce each) slices
    LAND O LAKES® Chedarella®
    or American Cheese
8   ounces thinly sliced deli turkey
    breast
8   slices tomato
2   thin slices onion, separated
    into rings

1. Carefully slice bread in half
crosswise. Spread dressing on top
and bottom halves of bread.

2. To assemble, place 6 lettuce
leaves on bottom bread half; layer
with all remaining ingredients. Top
with remaining lettuce leaves and
bread half. Secure with toothpicks.
Cut into wedges.

Nutrition Facts *(1 serving): Calories 420; Protein 24 g;*
Carbohydrate 28 g; Dietary Fiber 1 g; Fat 23 g;
Cholesterol 50 mg; Sodium 1400 mg

*Substitute 1 (1-pound) loaf Italian
bread.

Smoked Turkey Melts with Apple-Pepper Relish

*Smoked turkey, Swiss cheese
and a spicy apple-pepper relish
make an unbeatable hot sandwich
combination.*

Preparation time: 20 minutes
Grilling time: 4 minutes

[4 sandwiches]

RELISH
1/2 cup chopped apple
1/2 cup chopped red pepper
2   tablespoons sliced green onion
1 1/2 teaspoons red wine vinegar
1 1/2 teaspoons olive *or* vegetable oil
2-3 dashes hot pepper sauce

SANDWICH
4   slices Vienna bread
4   teaspoons mayonnaise
8   ounces thinly sliced deli
    smoked turkey breast
4   (3/4-ounce each) slices
    LAND O LAKES® Swiss Cheese

1. Prepare grill; heat until coals are
ash white. Stir together all relish
ingredients in small bowl; set
aside.

2. Lightly toast *1 side* of bread on
grill.

3. To assemble each sandwich,
layer toasted side of bread with
1 teaspoon mayonnaise, *1/4* turkey,
2 tablespoons relish and *1 slice*
cheese.

4. Place sandwiches on grill. Grill,
turning once, until sandwiches are
heated through and cheese is
melted (4 to 6 minutes). Serve with
remaining relish.

Nutrition Facts *(1 sandwich): Calories 270; Protein*
21 g; Carbohydrate 17 g; Dietary Fiber 1 g; Fat 13 g;
Cholesterol 45 mg; Sodium 1050 mg

Oven Directions: Heat oven to
350°. Stir together all relish
ingredients in small bowl; set
aside. Place toasted bread slices
on ungreased baking sheet; spread
with mayonnaise. Assemble
sandwiches as directed above.
Bake for 8 to 10 minutes or until
heated through and cheese is
melted. Serve with remaining
relish.

Focaccia Hero

Really Deviled Eggs

Hot mustard and two kinds of peppers provide the "heat" in these deviled eggs.

Preparation time: 20 minutes
Chilling time: 1 hour

[12 servings]

6	hard-cooked eggs, peeled
1/4	cup LAND O LAKES® Light *or* Fat Free Sour Cream
1/4	cup light mayonnaise
1/4	teaspoon salt
1/4	teaspoon ground red pepper
2	tablespoons sweet hot mustard
1/2	teaspoon hot pepper sauce
1/4	cup sliced green onions

1. Slice eggs in half lengthwise; remove egg yolks. Set egg white halves aside.

2. Mash egg yolks in medium bowl. Add all remaining ingredients *except* green onions; mix well. Stir in green onions.

3. Spoon about *1 rounded tablespoonful* egg yolk mixture into each egg white half. Garnish with additional sliced green onions, if desired. Cover; refrigerate at least 1 hour.

Nutrition Facts (1 serving): Calories 60; Protein 4 g; Carbohydrate 2 g; Dietary Fiber 0 g; Fat 4 g; Cholesterol 110 mg; Sodium 170 mg

South of the Border Potato Skins

Sausage, beans and cheese turn potato skins into a meal.

Preparation time: 30 minutes
Baking time: 4 minutes

[64 appetizers]

POTATOES

8	large baking potatoes, baked

FILLING

1 1/2	cups chopped onion
3/4	cup chopped green pepper
1	pound bulk pork sausage
1	cup water
1	(15-ounce) can hot chili beans, drained
1	(1 1/4-ounce) package taco seasoning mix
1/3	cup fresh chopped cilantro
1	(16-ounce) container LAND O LAKES® Light Sour Cream
3/4	teaspoon garlic powder
8	ounces (2 cups) LAND O LAKES® Cheddar Cheese, shredded

TOPPINGS

Guacamole, if desired
Ripe olives, if desired
Salsa, if desired

1. Cut each potato into quarters lengthwise; cut each quarter in half, making 8 pieces. Scoop out potato, leaving 1/4 inch shell. Place potato skins on ungreased baking sheets; set aside.

2. Place onion, green pepper and sausage in large skillet. Cook over medium-high heat, stirring occasionally, until sausage is browned (5 to 7 minutes). Stir in water, chili beans and taco seasoning mix. Reduce heat to low. Cook until flavors are blended (5 to 7 minutes).

3. *Heat oven to 375°.* Stir together cilantro, sour cream and garlic powder in small bowl.

4. Spoon *1 tablespoon* sausage filling into each potato skin; top with *2 teaspoons* cheese. Bake for 4 to 6 minutes or until cheese is melted. Dollop with sour cream mixture.

5. Garnish with guacamole, olives and salsa, if desired.

Nutrition Facts (1 appetizer): Calories 50; Protein 3 g; Carbohydrate 3 g; Dietary Fiber 0 g; Fat 3 g; Cholesterol 10 mg; Sodium 135 mg

TIP To save time, bake and scoop out the potatoes and prepare the filling a day ahead, and refrigerate. Assemble and bake just before serving.

What differentiates the muffuletta from ordinary heroes is its pungent topping, a marinated mixture of salty green olives, garlic, pimientos, capers, parsley, and herbs.

Muffuletta Loaf

Pack along this Southern-style sandwich for a leisurely picnic in the park.

Preparation time: 30 minutes
Chilling time: 5 hours

[6 servings]

¾ cup chopped stuffed green olives
¼ cup finely chopped fresh parsley
¼ cup olive *or* vegetable oil
1 (2-ounce) jar pimientos, drained, chopped
1 tablespoon capers, drained
1½ teaspoons finely chopped fresh oregano leaves
1½ teaspoons finely chopped fresh garlic
¼ teaspoon pepper
1 (11-inch) loaf unsliced Vienna bread*
5 slices (1-ounce each) bologna

6 ounces LAND O LAKES® Cheddar Cheese, cut into 16 slices
6 slices (¾-ounce each) salami
6 ounces LAND O LAKES® Monterey Jack Cheese, cut into 16 slices

1. Combine olives, parsley, oil, pimientos, capers, oregano, garlic and pepper in medium bowl. Cover; refrigerate 4 hours or overnight.

2. Drain olive mixture; *reserve marinade.* Set aside.

3. Carefully slice bread in half crosswise; remove bread in center, leaving ½-inch thick shells. Brush insides of shells generously with reserved marinade. Spoon *half* of olive mixture into bottom shell; press firmly. Layer bottom shell with bologna, cheddar cheese, salami and Monterey Jack cheese. Top with remaining olive mixture and remaining bread shell.

4. Wrap in aluminum foil. Refrigerate at least 1 hour.

5. To serve, cut into slices; secure with toothpicks.

<u>Nutrition Facts</u> *(1 serving): Calories 640; Protein 27 g; Carbohydrate 41 g; Dietary Fiber 3 g; Fat 41 g; Cholesterol 85 mg; Sodium 1650 mg*

*Substitute 1 (1-pound) unsliced loaf Italian bread.

Blue Cheese Tomato Tart

Cut into wedges, thie quiche-like tart makes an elegant appetizer or first course.

Preparation time: 30 minutes
Baking time: 37 minutes

[16 servings]

PASTRY

1½ cups all-purpose flour
6   tablespoons cold
    LAND O LAKES® Butter
4-5 tablespoons ice water

FILLING

1   (8-ounce) package cream
    cheese, softened
¼   cup crumbled blue cheese
¼   cup whipping cream
1   egg
1   tablespoon lemon juice
1   teaspoon grated lemon zest
½   teaspoon chopped fresh thyme
    leaves*
¼   teaspoon coarsely ground
    pepper
1   medium tomato, cut into
    6 (¼-inch) slices
1   teaspoon chopped fresh
    rosemary leaves**

    Rosemary sprigs, if desired
    Crumbled blue cheese, if
    desired

1. Heat oven to 375°. Place flour in large bowl; cut in butter until crumbly. Mix in water with fork just until moistened. Form into ball.

2. Roll out dough on lightly floured surface to 12-inch circle. Place in 11-inch tart pan, pressing firmly against bottom and sides of pan. Cut away excess pastry. Prick with fork. Bake for 17 to 22 minutes or until very lightly browned.

3. Meanwhile, combine cream cheese and blue cheese in large mixer bowl. Beat at medium speed, scraping bowl often, until creamy (1 to 2 minutes). Continue beating, gradually adding whipping cream and egg, until blended (1 to 2 minutes). Stir in all remaining ingredients *except* tomato and rosemary.

4. Spread into baked pastry. Arrange tomato slices on filling; sprinkle with rosemary.

5. Bake for 20 to 25 minutes or until filling is set. Let stand 20 minutes; serve warm. Garnish with additional rosemary and crumbled blue cheese, if desired.

Nutrition Facts (1 serving): Calories 160; Protein 3 g; Carbohydrate 10 g; Dietary Fiber 0 g; Fat 12 g; Cholesterol 45 mg; Sodium 120 mg

*Substitute ½ teaspoon dried thyme leaves.

**Substitute ½ teaspoon dried rosemary leaves, crushed.

Blue Cheese Tomato Tart

Fiesta Spread

Sour cream, cream cheese and salsa blend together for an easy and colorful appetizer.

Preparation time: 10 minutes
Chilling time: 1 hour

[10 servings]

¼ cup LAND O LAKES® Fat Free Sour Cream
1 (8-ounce) package nonfat cream cheese, softened
2 ounces (¼ cup) LAND O LAKES® Cheddar Cheese, shredded
3 tablespoons chopped jalapeño peppers*
½ cup thick and chunky salsa

1. Combine sour cream and cream cheese in small mixer bowl. Beat, scraping bowl often, until smooth (1 to 2 minutes). Add cheddar cheese and peppers; mix well.

2. Spread cream cheese mixture onto bottom of 10-inch round serving plate. Cover; refrigerate at least 1 hour.

3. Just before serving, spread evenly with salsa; top with remaining cheese. Serve with tortilla chips.

Nutrition Facts *(1 tablespoon without chips): Calories 40; Protein 4 g; Carbohydrate 3 g; Dietary Fiber 0 g; Fat 1 g; Cholesterol 5 mg; Sodium 290 mg*

*Substitute 3 tablespoons chopped mild green chilies and ½ teaspoon ground cumin.

TIP For convenience, look for jars of red chopped jalapeño peppers in the produce section of the supermarket.

Vegetarian Pizza

Italian bread shells, also known as Boboli, make easy crusts for these pizzas topped with garden-fresh green pepper and Roma tomatoes.

Preparation time: 35 minutes
Baking time: 10 minutes

[4 servings]

2 teaspoons LAND O LAKES® Butter
2 medium (1 cup) onions, quartered lengthwise, sliced ⅛-inch
2 teaspoons purchased minced garlic
¼ teaspoon crushed red pepper
1 small (1 cup) green pepper, cut into ¼-inch strips
6 ounces (1½ cups) LAND O LAKES® Mozzarella Cheese, shredded
4 (6-inch) individual round pre-baked Italian bread shells *or* focaccia
3 medium Roma tomatoes, sliced ¼-inch
¼ cup sliced ripe olives, if desired

1. Heat oven to 425°. Melt butter in 10-inch nonstick skillet until sizzling; stir in onions, garlic and red pepper. Cook over low heat, stirring occasionally, until onions are very soft and golden (15 minutes). Add pepper strips. Continue cooking, stirring constantly, until peppers are crisply tender (5 minutes).

2. Sprinkle *1 cup* cheese evenly over bread shells to within ½ inch of edge; top with onion mixture, tomatoes and olives.

3. Sprinkle with remaining cheese. Bake for 10 to 12 minutes or until cheese is melted and pizza is heated through.

Nutrition Facts *(1 serving): Calories 480; Protein 27 g; Carbohydrate 59 g; Dietary Fiber 4 g; Fat 16 g; Cholesterol 35 mg; Sodium 850 mg*

Philly Cheese Steak Wraps

Beef, cheese and peppers become a modern classic when served in a warm tortilla.

Preparation time: 20 minutes
Microwaving time: 1 minute

[6 sandwiches]

3	tablespoons LAND O LAKES® Butter
2	cups thinly sliced onion rings, cut in half, separated
1½	cups red pepper strips, cut 2x¼-inch
1½	cups green pepper strips, cut 2x¼-inch
12	slices (¾-ounce each) LAND O LAKES® American Cheese, cut into strips
6	ounces thinly sliced deli roast beef, cut into 2x½-inch strips
½	teaspoon garlic salt
6	(10-inch) flour tortillas, warmed

1. Melt butter in 10-inch skillet until sizzling; add onions and peppers. Cook over medium-high heat, stirring occasionally, until onions are golden (6 to 8 minutes). Remove from heat. Stir in cheese, beef strips and garlic salt.

2. Place about *1 cup* filling in center of each warm tortilla. Fold two opposite edges of tortilla toward center over filling. Roll up open end of tortilla toward opposite edge. Place on microwave-safe plate, seam-side down.

3. Microwave two tortillas on HIGH, turning or rearranging after half the time, until heated through (1 to 2 minutes). Repeat with remaining tortillas.

Nutrition Facts (1 sandwich): Calories 470; Protein 23 g; Carbohydrate 39 g; Dietary Fiber 3 g; Fat 25 g; Cholesterol 80 mg; Sodium 770 mg

[kitchen notes]

Named for its city of origin, the legendary Philadelphia steak sandwich
has enjoyed many interpretations over the years.
Traditional Philly steak is sliced thin and piled extra high on a hoagie bun.
Layers of cheese ooze out the sides, and it's often as sloppy
as it is delicious. This version keeps the flavor while eliminating
the mess by wrapping everything up
in a flour tortilla.

Cheese & Mushroom Oven Omelet

Cheddar cheese, bacon and mushrooms fill this delicious breakfast entrée.

Preparation time: 20 minutes
Baking time: 20 minutes

[6 servings]

2   tablespoons LAND O LAKES® Butter
8   ounces (2 cups) sliced fresh mushrooms*
⅓   cup milk
6   eggs
2   tablespoons all-purpose flour
⅛   teaspoon pepper
6   ounces (1½ cups) LAND O LAKES® Cheddar Cheese, shredded
6   slices (¼ cup) crisply cooked bacon, crumbled

1. Heat oven to 350°. Melt butter until sizzling in 10-inch skillet; add mushrooms. Cook over medium heat, stirring occasionally, until mushrooms are tender (4 to 6 minutes). Drain. Set aside.

2. Combine milk, eggs, flour and pepper in medium bowl. Beat with wire whisk until frothy. Stir in mushrooms, *1 cup* cheese and bacon.

3. Pour egg mixture into buttered 8-inch square baking pan; sprinkle with remaining cheese. Bake for 20 to 25 minutes or until eggs are set in center.

Nutrition Facts (1 serving): Calories 290; Protein 16 g; Carbohydrate 6 g; Dietary Fiber 1 g; Fat 22 g; Cholesterol 260 mg; Sodium 410 mg

* Substitute 1 (4-ounce) can sliced mushrooms, drained.

MICROWAVE DIRECTIONS:
Microwave butter in 9-inch pie plate on HIGH (30 to 40 seconds). Stir in mushrooms. Cover with plastic food wrap; microwave on HIGH, stirring after half the time, until mushrooms are tender (2 to 3 minutes). Drain; set aside. Combine eggs, milk, flour and pepper in medium bowl. Beat egg mixture with wire whisk until frothy. Stir in mushrooms, *1 cup* cheese and bacon. Pour into same pie plate. Microwave on HIGH, stirring after half the time, until eggs are set in center (3½ to 5½ minutes). Sprinkle with remaining cheese. Let stand 2 minutes.

Toasted Onion Cheese Log

Caramelized onion adds rich flavor to this hors d'oeuvre.

Preparation time: 20 minutes
Chilling time: 3 hours

[32 servings]

1   tablespoon LAND O LAKES® Butter
¾   cup finely chopped onion
1   (8-ounce) package cream cheese, softened
6   ounces (1½ cups) LAND O LAKES® American Cheese *or* Cheddar Cheese, shredded
2   tablespoons chopped fresh parsley
⅛   teaspoon pepper

⅓   cup chopped fresh parsley, if desired
   Assorted crackers

1. Melt butter in 8-inch skillet until sizzling; add onion. Cook over medium heat, stirring occasionally, until onion is golden brown (10 to 14 minutes). Cool completely.

2. Stir cream cheese in medium bowl until smooth. Add onion and all remaining ingredients *except* ⅓ cup parsley and crackers; mix well.

3. Spoon mixture onto waxed paper. Refrigerate for 1 hour.

4. Shape cheese mixture into 10-inch log; roll in ⅓ cup parsley to coat. Wrap in plastic food wrap; refrigerate at least 2 hours.

5. Serve with crackers. Store refrigerated.

Nutrition Facts (1 tablespoon without crackers): Calories 50; Protein 2 g; Carbohydrate <1 g; Dietary Fiber 0 g; Fat 4.5 g; Cholesterol 15 mg; Sodium 100 mg

Cheese & Mushroom Oven Omelet

Italian Nachos

A tasty change of pace from traditional Mexican nachos.

Preparation time: 20 minutes
Baking time: 5 minutes

[8 servings]

1	(10-ounce) container refrigerated four cheese *or* Alfredo sauce, warmed
¼	teaspoon crushed red pepper
8	ounces white corn tortilla chips
4	ounces hot Italian sausage, cooked
4	ounces (1 cup) LAND O LAKES® Mozzarella Cheese, shredded
½	cup chopped tomato
¼	cup sliced green onions
1	(2¼-ounce) can sliced, pitted ripe olives

1. Heat oven to 450°. Combine cheese sauce and red pepper in small bowl.

2. Spread *half* of tortilla chips on ovenproof platter; top with *half* cheese sauce, *half* Italian sausage and *half* mozzarella cheese. Repeat with remaining chips, cheese sauce, sausage and cheese.

3. Bake for 5 minutes or until cheese is melted. Top with remaining ingredients. Serve immediately.

Nutrition Facts *(1 serving): Calories 330; Protein 11 g; Carbohydrate 21 g; Dietary Fiber 2 g; Fat 24 g; Cholesterol 35 mg; Sodium 680 mg*

Tex-Mex Layered Dip

Your guests will make this classic and colorful dip disappear in no time.

Preparation time: 15 minutes

[24 servings]

2	(15-ounce) cans pinto beans, rinsed, drained
1	(16-ounce) carton LAND O LAKES® Fat Free Sour Cream
1	(1¼-ounce) package taco seasoning mix
1½	cups finely shredded lettuce
1	large tomato, chopped
¼	cup sliced green onions
2	ounces (½ cup) LAND O LAKES® Cheddar Cheese, finely shredded
¼	cup sliced ripe olives

Carrot and celery sticks *or* Baked tortilla chips

1. Mash beans in medium bowl; stir in *1 cup* sour cream and taco seasoning mix.

2. Spread bean mixture on large serving plate. Spread remaining sour cream over bean mixture. Sprinkle with lettuce, tomato, green onions, cheese and olives. Refrigerate until serving time.

3. Serve with carrot and celery sticks or chips.

Nutrition Facts *(1 serving dip only): Calories 60; Protein 4 g; Carbohydrate 10 g; Dietary Fiber 4 g; Fat 1 g; Cholesterol 5 mg; Sodium 150 mg*

Orange Burst Fruit Dip

This lowfat dip is creamy and smooth with a hint of orange.

Preparation time: 15 minutes
Chilling time: 30 minutes

[2 cups]

¼	cup sugar
¼	cup orange juice
2	cups LAND O LAKES® Fat Free Sour Cream
1	tablespoon grated orange zest

1. Stir together all dip ingredients in small bowl. Cover; refrigerate at least 30 minutes.

2. Serve with fresh fruit.

Nutrition Facts *(1 tablespoon dip without fruit): Calories 19; Protein 31 g; Carbohydrate 4 g; Dietary Fiber 0 g; Fat 0 g; Cholesterol 1 mg; Sodium 15 mg*

Fruit and cheese, like many classic combinations, is a harmonious interplay of opposites: crunchy and creamy, salty and sweet.

Cinnamon 'n Cheese Apple Dip

Serve this cinnamon-flavored cream cheese and Chedarella® cheese dip with a variety of apple or pear slices.

Preparation time: 10 minutes

[12 servings]

4   ounces nonfat cream cheese, softened
1   cup LAND O LAKES® Fat Free Sour Cream
2   teaspoons sugar
½   teaspoon ground cinnamon
¼   teaspoon ground nutmeg

3   ounces (¾ cup) LAND O LAKES® Chedarella® Cheese, shredded
2   red *and/or* green apples, sliced
     Lemon juice

1. Beat cream cheese in small mixer bowl on medium speed, scraping bowl often, until smooth. Add sour cream, sugar, cinnamon and nutmeg. Continue beating until light and fluffy (2 to 3 minutes).

2. Spread mixture on large platter into 10-inch circle. Top with Chedarella® cheese. Sprinkle cut edges of apples with lemon juice to prevent browning. Arrange apple slices around dip.

Nutrition Facts (2 tablespoons dip with apples): Calories 70; Protein 4 g; Carbohydrate 9 g; Dietary Fiber 1 g; Fat 2.5 g; Cholesterol 10 mg; Sodium 120 mg

Oven-Baked Chicken Wings

These oven-baked chicken wings are battered for crunch and full of flavor.

Preparation time: 30 minutes
Baking time: 40 minutes

[3 dozen appetizers]

⅔   cup all-purpose baking mix, pancake mix *or* all-purpose flour
1   tablespoon paprika
2   teaspoons garlic salt
1   teaspoon coarsely ground pepper
2   tablespoons LAND O LAKES® Butter, melted
3   pounds chicken wings, each wing cut into 3 parts (discard tips)

1   cup barbecue sauce, warmed

1. Heat oven to 425°. Stir together baking mix, paprika, garlic salt and pepper in small bowl. Coat chicken wings with paprika mixture.

2. Melt butter in 15x10x1-inch jelly-roll pan in oven (3 to 5 minutes). Place chicken wings in pan, turning to coat with butter.

3. Bake for 40 to 45 minutes, turning chicken wings after 20 minutes, or until no longer pink. Serve chicken wings with barbecue sauce.

Nutrition Facts (1 appetizer): Calories 55; Protein 4 g; Carbohydrate 3 g; Dietary Fiber 0 g; Fat 4 g; Cholesterol 10 mg; Sodium 180 mg

Southwestern Quesadillas

These chicken and cheese appetizer quesadillas can also be served for lunch or supper with slices of fresh fruit.

Preparation time: 30 minutes
Baking time: 10 minutes

[18 servings]

FILLING

⅓	cup mayonnaise
⅓	cup LAND O LAKES® Light Sour Cream
4	ounces (1 cup) sliced deli chicken breast, cut into small pieces
4	ounces (1 cup) LAND O LAKES® Chedarella® Cheese, shredded
2	tablespoons sliced green onions
2	tablespoons chopped mild green chilies, drained
½	teaspoon grated lime zest
3	drops hot pepper sauce

TORTILLAS

6	(8-inch) flour tortillas
1	tablespoon LAND O LAKES® Butter, melted
	Cayenne pepper *or* chili powder

TOPPINGS

LAND O LAKES® Light Sour Cream
Salsa
Lime wedges

1. Heat oven to 375°. Stir together all filling ingredients in large bowl.

2. Spread about ⅓ *cup* cheese mixture on *one half* of each tortilla; fold other side of tortilla over cheese mixture. Brush both sides of each tortilla with butter; sprinkle top with cayenne pepper. Place on large baking sheet. Repeat with remaining tortillas.

3. Bake for 10 to 15 minutes or until heated through.

4. Cut each quesadilla into three wedges. Serve with desired toppings. Garnish with lime wedges.

Nutrition Facts (1 serving): Calories 110; Protein 5 g; Carbohydrate 7 g; Dietary Fiber 0 g; Fat 7 g; Cholesterol 15 mg; Sodium 140 mg

Vegetable & Cheese Focaccia

This flavorful vegetable sandwich makes a great lunch or light supper.

Preparation time: 15 minutes
Cooking time: 6 minutes

[6 sandwiches]

1	tablespoon olive *or* vegetable oil
2	medium carrots, thinly sliced
½	cup thinly sliced red onion
1	medium red *or* yellow pepper, cut into 2x⅛-inch strips
1	medium zucchini, sliced ⅛-inch
1	tablespoon chopped fresh basil leaves*
1	(9 to 12-inch) pre-baked round focaccia *or* Italian bread shell, cut in half crosswise
6	(¾-ounce each) slices LAND O LAKES® Provolone Cheese

1. Heat oil in 10-inch skillet; add carrots. Cook over medium heat 2 minutes. Add all remaining ingredients *except* focaccia and cheese. Continue cooking, stirring occasionally, until vegetables are crisply tender (4 to 6 minutes).

2. Place cheese on bottom half of focaccia; top with vegetable mixture. Place top half of focaccia over vegetables to form sandwich. Cut into 6 wedges; serve warm or at room temperature.

Nutrition Facts (1 sandwich) Calories 330; Protein 15 g; Carbohydrate 38 g; Dietary Fiber 2 g; Fat 12 g; Cholesterol 20 mg; Sodium 590 mg

*Substitute 1 teaspoon dried basil leaves.

Southwestern Quesadillas

Chicken Salad Wraps

Wrap up pre-made salad, veggies and cheese for a meal when it's too hot to cook.

Preparation time: 20 minutes

[4 sandwiches]

4	(10-inch) flour tortillas, warmed
1	pint (2 cups) deli chicken *or* seafood salad
8	slices tomato, each cut in half
8	(¾-ounce each) slices LAND O LAKES® American Cheese, cut into strips
8	leaves leaf lettuce

1. To serve, spread warm tortilla with *½ cup* chicken salad; layer with *¼* tomato, *¼* cheese and *2* lettuce leaves.

2. Fold two opposite edges of tortilla toward center over filling. Roll up open end of tortilla toward opposite edge. Repeat with remaining tortillas.

Nutrition Facts (1 sandwich): Calories 600; Protein 24 g; Carbohydrate 39 g; Dietary Fiber 3 g; Fat 39 g; Cholesterol 80 mg; Sodium 1030 mg

TIP The flour tortillas used to wrap this chicken salad make a great replacement for sandwich bread. Try wrapping any of your favorite sandwich fillings.

Pineapple Glazed Riblets

Horseradish adds spark to these tender riblets.

Preparation time: 25 minutes
Baking time: 45 minutes

[72 riblets]

SAUCE

½	cup honey
2	(8-ounce) cans crushed pineapple
1	tablespoon cornstarch
3	tablespoons cider vinegar
2	tablespoons soy sauce
1	tablespoon prepared horseradish
1	teaspoon finely chopped fresh garlic

MEAT

3	pounds pork riblets

1. Stir together all sauce ingredients in large bowl.

2. *Heat oven to 425°.* Place riblets in lightly greased 15x10x1-inch jelly-roll pan. Bake for 15 minutes. Drain off fat.

3. *Reduce heat to 400°.* Pour sauce over riblets. Bake for 45 to 55 minutes or until tender, stirring occasionally.

MICROWAVE DIRECTIONS

Stir together all sauce ingredients in large bowl. Microwave on HIGH, stirring twice during last half of time, until mixture is slightly thickened and heated through 4½ to 5 minutes. Set aside. Place half of riblets spaced at least ½-inch apart on 9-inch round serving dish. Cover with waxed paper; microwave on HIGH, turning dish ¼ turn twice, until fork tender (8 to 9 minutes). Repeat with remaining riblets.

Nutrition Facts (1 riblet): Calories 60; Protein 5 g; Carbohydrate 3 g; Dietary Fiber 0; Fat 2.5 g; Cholesterol 15 mg; Sodium 40 mg

Chicken Salad Wraps

Bread Board

Muffins and coffee cakes are exactly right when you're hungry for baked goods that are sweet, but not too sweet. To introduce warm-from-the-oven flavor to the main course, this chapter also includes Three-Grain Whole Wheat Bread and other hearty home-baked favorites.

Irish Soda Bread

Technique

Over-mixing of the batter can make quick breads tough. To keep coffee cakes, scones and muffins tender and light, combine dry and wet ingredients as quickly as possible. When you see no more dry bits of flour, you're done; don't worry about remaining lumps.

Store baked bread wrapped in waxed paper (plastic makes the crust soggy) on the counter for up to four or five days; large loaves keep better than small ones.

Baked bread, muffins and coffee cakes can also be frozen, tightly wrapped in plastic food wrap and placed in a resealable freezer bag. To revive, unwrap and thaw, then place the in a preheated 350 degree oven for 5 to 10 minutes until warm.

Irish Soda Bread

This traditional Irish round quick bread is leavened with baking soda.

Preparation time: 15 minutes
Baking time: 30 minutes

[1 loaf; 12 servings]

2½   cups all-purpose flour
3   tablespoons sugar
2   teaspoons baking powder
1   teaspoon baking soda
½   teaspoon salt
⅓   cup cold LAND O LAKES® Butter
1¼   cups buttermilk*
½   cup currants *or* raisins

1. Heat oven to 375°. Stir together flour, sugar, baking powder, baking soda and salt in large bowl; cut in butter until crumbly. Stir in buttermilk and currants just until moistened.

2. Place on lightly floured surface; knead gently 10 times. Shape into ball. Place on greased baking sheet. Pat into 6-inch circle. Cut ½-inch deep "X" in top of dough with sharp knife.

3. Bake for 30 to 35 minutes or until golden brown. Serve warm.

Nutrition Facts (1 serving): Calories 180; Protein 4 g; Carbohydrate 30 g; Dietary Fiber 1 g; Fat 6 g; Cholesterol 15 mg; Sodium 360 mg

*Substitute 4 teaspoons vinegar plus enough milk to equal 1¼ cups.

Parmesan Butter Pan Biscuits

A savory blend of Parmesan and basil update these country-style pan biscuits.

Preparation time: 15 minutes
Baking time: 25 minutes

[1 dozen biscuits]

⅓   cup LAND O LAKES® Butter
2¼   cups all-purpose flour
2   tablespoons freshly grated Parmesan cheese
1   tablespoon baking powder
1   tablespoon sugar
1   tablespoon chopped fresh parsley
1   teaspoon dried basil leaves
1   cup milk

1. Heat oven to 400°. Melt butter in 8-inch square baking pan in oven (3 to 5 minutes).

2. Meanwhile, combine all ingredients *except* milk in medium bowl. Stir in milk just until moistened.

3. Turn dough onto lightly floured surface; knead 10 times or until smooth. Roll dough into 12x4-inch rectangle. Cut into 12 (1-inch) strips.

4. Dip each strip into melted butter. Place in same pan. Bake for 25 to 30 minutes or until lightly browned.

Nutrition Facts (1 biscuit): Calories 150; Protein 4 g; Carbohydrate 20 g; Dietary Fiber 0 g; Fat 6 g; Cholesterol 15 mg; Sodium 170 mg

Irish Soda Bread

Technique

Over-mixing of the batter can make quick breads tough. To keep coffee cakes, scones and muffins tender and light, combine dry and wet ingredients as quickly as possible. When you see no more dry bits of flour, you're done; don't worry about remaining lumps.

Store baked bread wrapped in waxed paper (plastic makes the crust soggy) on the counter for up to four or five days; large loaves keep better than small ones.

Baked bread, muffins and coffee cakes can also be frozen, tightly wrapped in plastic food wrap and placed in a resealable freezer bag. To revive, unwrap and thaw, then place the in a preheated 350 degree oven for 5 to 10 minutes until warm.

Irish Soda Bread

This traditional Irish round quick bread is leavened with baking soda.

Preparation time: 15 minutes
Baking time: 30 minutes

[1 loaf; 12 servings]

2½ cups all-purpose flour
3   tablespoons sugar
2   teaspoons baking powder
1   teaspoon baking soda
½   teaspoon salt
⅓   cup cold LAND O LAKES®
     Butter
1¼ cups buttermilk*
½   cup currants *or* raisins

1. Heat oven to 375°. Stir together flour, sugar, baking powder, baking soda and salt in large bowl; cut in butter until crumbly. Stir in buttermilk and currants just until moistened.

2. Place on lightly floured surface; knead gently 10 times. Shape into ball. Place on greased baking sheet. Pat into 6-inch circle. Cut ½-inch deep "X" in top of dough with sharp knife.

3. Bake for 30 to 35 minutes or until golden brown. Serve warm.

Nutrition Facts (1 serving): Calories 180; Protein 4 g; Carbohydrate 30 g; Dietary Fiber 1 g; Fat 6 g; Cholesterol 15 mg; Sodium 360 mg

*Substitute 4 teaspoons vinegar plus enough milk to equal 1¼ cups.

Parmesan Butter Pan Biscuits

A savory blend of Parmesan and basil update these country-style pan biscuits.

Preparation time: 15 minutes
Baking time: 25 minutes

[1 dozen biscuits]

⅓   cup LAND O LAKES® Butter
2¼ cups all-purpose flour
2   tablespoons freshly grated
     Parmesan cheese
1   tablespoon baking powder
1   tablespoon sugar
1   tablespoon chopped fresh
     parsley
1   teaspoon dried basil leaves
1   cup milk

1. Heat oven to 400°. Melt butter in 8-inch square baking pan in oven (3 to 5 minutes).

2. Meanwhile, combine all ingredients *except* milk in medium bowl. Stir in milk just until moistened.

3. Turn dough onto lightly floured surface; knead 10 times or until smooth. Roll dough into 12x4-inch rectangle. Cut into 12 (1-inch) strips.

4. Dip each strip into melted butter. Place in same pan. Bake for 25 to 30 minutes or until lightly browned.

Nutrition Facts (1 biscuit): Calories 150; Protein 4 g; Carbohydrate 20 g; Dietary Fiber 0 g; Fat 6 g; Cholesterol 15 mg; Sodium 170 mg

Whole Wheat Pizza Dough

Add your favorite fresh toppings for a pizza that's far better than delivery.

Preparation time: 25 minutes
Rising time: 45 minutes
Baking time: 17 minutes

[12 servings]

DOUGH

1½-2	cups all-purpose flour
2	tablespoons LAND O LAKES® Butter, softened
1	(¼-ounce) package active dry yeast
1	tablespoon sugar
1	teaspoon salt
1	cup hot water (120° to 130°F)
1	cup whole wheat flour

TOPPINGS

Finely chopped fresh garlic
Fresh oregano leaves
Fresh tomato slices
Sliced mushrooms
Pitted ripe olives
Sliced onions
LAND O LAKES® Mozzarella Cheese, shredded

1. Combine 1½ cups flour, butter, yeast, sugar and salt in large mixer bowl; stir to blend. Add hot water. Beat at medium speed, scraping bowl occasionally, until smooth (2 to 3 minutes) Stir in whole wheat flour and enough remaining flour by hand to make dough easy to handle.

2. Turn dough onto lightly floured surface; knead until smooth and elastic (3 to 5 minutes). Place in greased bowl; turn greased-side up. Cover; let rise in warm place until double in size (45 to 60 minutes).

3. *Heat oven to 400°.* Punch down dough; divide in half. Press each half with lightly floured hands into greased 12-inch pizza pan.

4. Bake for 5 minutes. Add choice of toppings, as desired. Continue baking for 12 to 15 minutes or until crust is golden brown.

Nutrition Facts (1 serving dough only): Calories 110; Protein 3 g; Carbohydrate 20 g; Dietary Fiber 2 g; Fat 2.5 g; Cholesterol 5 mg; Sodium 200 mg

[kitchen notes]

If you're using a food processor to make quick work of kneading, spritz the blade with no-stick cooking spray before you begin. This will prevent the dough from clinging to the blade during the kneading process.

To effectively knead dough by hand, use the heels of your hands to press down and away. Then fold the dough and turn it slightly, repeating the press-fold-turn actions several times. Dough is properly kneaded when its texture is smooth.

Tender Popovers

You'll need a popover pan or custard cups for these old-fashioned favorites.

Preparation time: 10 minutes
Baking time: 35 minutes

[6 popovers]

3   eggs
1¼ cups milk
1¼ cups all-purpose flour
¼   teaspoon salt

1. Heat oven to 450°. Grease popover pan or six (6-ounce) custard cups. Place in oven for 5 minutes.

2. Meanwhile, beat eggs in small mixer bowl at medium speed, scraping bowl often, until light and lemon-colored (1 to 2 minutes). Add milk; continue beating 1 minute. Add flour and salt; beat until well mixed (1 to 2 minutes).

3. Pour batter into prepared popover pan or custard cups. Bake for 15 minutes. *Reduce temperature to 350°. (DO NOT OPEN OVEN DOOR.)* Bake for 20 to 25 minutes or until golden brown. Insert knife in popovers to allow steam to escape. Serve immediately.

Nutrition Facts (1 popover): Calories 160; Protein 8 g; Carbohydrate 23 g; Dietary Fiber 1 g; Fat 3.5 g; Cholesterol 110 mg; Sodium 150 mg

TIP Eggs and milk should be at room temperature (72°F) to help ensure successful popovers. Use solid shortening to grease pan rather than no stick cooking spray.

TIP Perfect popovers are never underbaked; always bake them for the allotted time and resist the urge to peek while they are baking. Opening the oven door exposes the popovers to cool air, which can cause them to fall. To prevent sogginess, prick freshly baked popovers with a fork or knife point to allow the steam to release.

Ginger Pear Coffee Bread

Pears give this bread a slightly sweet taste while crystallized ginger adds a hint of spice.

Preparation time: 30 minutes
Baking time: 40 minutes

[9 servings]

BREAD
2   cups all-purpose flour
1   cup firmly packed brown sugar
½   cup LAND O LAKES® Butter, softened
2   eggs
2   tablespoons lemon juice
2   teaspoons grated lemon zest
1½ teaspoons baking powder
½   teaspoon salt

1   medium (1 cup) ripe pear, peeled, cored, cut into ½-inch pieces
½   cup currants *or* raisins
¼   cup finely chopped crystallized ginger

TOPPING
1   medium pear, cored, sliced ⅛-inch
2   tablespoons firmly packed brown sugar
     Powdered sugar

1. Heat oven to 350°. Combine all bread ingredients *except* pear, currants and ginger in large mixer bowl. Beat at low speed, scraping bowl often, until well mixed (2 to 3 minutes). (Batter will be stiff.) Stir in pear pieces, currants and ginger by hand.

2. Spread batter into greased and floured 9-inch round cake pan. Arrange pear slices in circle over batter; sprinkle with 2 tablespoons brown sugar.

3. Bake for 40 to 50 minutes or until toothpick inserted in center comes out clean. Cool 10 minutes; remove from pan. Sprinkle with powdered sugar.

Nutrition Facts (1 serving): Calories 370; Protein 5 g; Carbohydrate 62 g; Dietary Fiber 2 g; Fat 12 g; Cholesterol 75 mg; Sodium 300 mg

Homemade bread comforts on many levels: savory and crusty or tinged with sweetness, the aroma, texture and taste satisfy like no purchased loaf can.

Maple Pecan Cornbread with Maple Butter

Serve this dense, flavorful cornbread warm with a generous helping of maple butter.

Preparation time: 20 minutes
Baking time: 25 minutes

[9 servings]

CORN BREAD

1	cup cornmeal
1	cup all-purpose flour
1	teaspoon baking powder
1	teaspoon baking soda
1/2	teaspoon salt
3	eggs
3	tablespoons LAND O LAKES® Butter, softened
2	tablespoons firmly packed brown sugar
3/4	cup buttermilk*
1/3	cup pure maple syrup *or* maple-flavored syrup
1	teaspoon maple flavoring
3/4	cup chopped pecans, toasted

MAPLE BUTTER

1/2	cup LAND O LAKES® Butter
1	tablespoon pure maple syrup or maple-flavored syrup
1	teaspoon maple flavoring

1. Heat oven to 350°. Combine cornmeal, flour, baking powder, baking soda and salt in small mixer bowl.

2. Combine eggs, 3 tablespoons butter and brown sugar in large mixer bowl. Beat at medium speed until well mixed (1 to 2 minutes).

3. Add buttermilk, 1/3 cup maple syrup and 1 teaspoon maple flavoring. Continue beating until well mixed (2 to 3 minutes). Reduce speed to low; add flour mixture. Beat, scraping bowl often, until well mixed (1 to 2 minutes). Stir in pecans by hand.

4. Spoon into greased 8-inch square baking pan. Bake for 25 to 30 minutes or until toothpick inserted in center comes out clean. (Corn bread may dip slightly in center.)

5. Meanwhile, combine all maple butter ingredients in small mixer bowl. Beat at medium speed until fluffy (2 to 3 minutes). Serve with warm cornbread.

Nutrition Facts (1 serving plus about 1 tablespoon Maple Butter): Calories 380; Protein 6 g; Carbohydrate 37 g; Dietary Fiber 2 g; Fat 23 g; Cholesterol 100 mg; Sodium 450 mg

*Substitute 2 teaspoons vinegar plus enough milk to equal 3/4 cup.

Lemon Poppy-Seed Bread

Everyone will enjoy these mini loaves of lemon-glazed bread.

Preparation time: 20 minutes
Baking time: 30 minutes

[4 mini loaves; 8 servings/loaf]

BREAD

2¼ cups all-purpose flour
1¼ cups sugar
1   cup LAND O LAKES® Butter, softened
¾   cup milk
3   eggs
2   tablespoons poppy seed
1   tablespoon grated lemon zest
1½   teaspoons baking powder
1   teaspoon salt

GLAZE

⅓   cup sugar
3   tablespoons LAND O LAKES® Butter, melted
4   teaspoons lemon juice

1. Heat oven to 350°. Grease bottom only of four (5½x3-inch) mini loaf pans. Set aside.

2. Combine all bread ingredients in large mixer bowl. Beat at medium speed, scraping bowl often, until well mixed.

3. Spread batter into prepared pans. Bake for 30 to 40 minutes or until toothpick inserted in center comes out clean.

4. Stir together all glaze ingredients in small bowl. Drizzle over warm bread loaves. Cool 10 minutes; remove from pans.

Nutrition Facts (1 serving): Calories 140; Protein 2 g; Carbohydrate 17 g; Dietary Fiber 0 g; Fat 8 g; Cholesterol 40 mg; Sodium 170 mg

Cranberry Orange Scones

Cranberries and orange add extra flavor to this English quick bread.

Preparation time: 30 minutes
Baking time: 10 minutes

[1 dozen scones]

SCONES

1¾   cups all-purpose flour
3   tablespoons sugar
2½   teaspoons baking powder
2   teaspoons grated orange zest
⅓   cup LAND O LAKES® Butter
½   cup dried cranberries
1   egg, beaten
4-6 tablespoons half-and-half

1   egg, beaten
2   tablespoons sugar

ORANGE BUTTER

½   cup LAND O LAKES® Butter, softened
2   tablespoons orange marmalade

1. Heat oven to 400°. Combine flour, 3 tablespoons sugar, baking powder and orange zest in medium bowl; cut in ⅓ cup butter until mixture resembles fine crumbs. Stir in cranberries, 1 egg and just enough half-and-half so dough leaves sides of bowl.

2. Turn dough onto lightly floured surface; knead lightly 10 times. Roll into 9-inch circle; cut into 12 wedges.

3. Place wedges on ungreased baking sheet. Brush with beaten egg; sprinkle each with *½ teaspoon* sugar. Bake for 10 to 12 minutes or until golden brown. Immediately remove from baking sheet.

4. Meanwhile, combine ½ cup butter and orange marmalade in small mixer bowl. Beat at medium speed, scraping bowl often, until well mixed (1 to 2 minutes). Serve with scones.

Nutrition Facts (1 scone with about 1 tablespoon Orange Butter): Calories 240; Protein 3 g; Carbohydrate 27 g; Dietary Fiber 1 g; Fat 14 g; Cholesterol 70 mg; Sodium 240 mg

Lemon Poppy-Seed Bread

Country Peach Coffee Cake

A crunchy oatmeal topping is a delightful finish to this moist peach coffee cake.

Preparation time: 30 minutes
Baking time: 1 hour
Cooling time: 1 hour

[15 servings]

FILLING

1   (21-ounce) can peach pie filling
1   (16-ounce) can peach slices in light syrup, well-drained

TOPPING

1   cup firmly packed brown sugar
1   cup all-purpose flour
½   cup quick-cooking oats
½   cup LAND O LAKES® Butter, softened

CAKE

1   cup sugar
1   cup LAND O LAKES® Butter, softened
1¼ cups LAND O LAKES® Sour Cream
2   eggs, slightly beaten
1   tablespoon vanilla
3   cups all-purpose flour
1   teaspoon baking powder
1   teaspoon baking soda
½   teaspoon salt

GLAZE

1   cup powdered sugar
1-2   tablespoons fat free milk

1. Heat oven to 350°. Stir together all filling ingredients in medium bowl; set aside.

2. Stir together all topping ingredients in medium bowl until crumbly; set aside.

3. Combine sugar and 1 cup butter in large mixer bowl. Beat at medium speed, scraping bowl often, until creamy (1 to 2 minutes). Add sour cream, eggs and vanilla. Continue beating, scraping bowl often, until well mixed (1 to 2 minutes). Reduce speed to low; add all remaining cake ingredients. Beat, scraping bowl often, until smooth (1 to 2 minutes).

4. Spread *half* of batter into greased 13x9-inch baking pan. Spread peach filling over batter. Drop spoonfuls of remaining batter over filling (do not spread). Sprinkle with topping. Bake for 60 to 70 minutes or until toothpick inserted in center comes out clean. Cool completely.

5. Stir together powdered sugar and enough milk for desired glazing consistency in small bowl. Drizzle over cooled coffee cake.

Nutrition Facts (1 serving): Calories 550; Protein 6 g; Carbohydrate 81 g; Dietary Fiber 2 g; Fat 23 g; Cholesterol 90 mg; Sodium 410 mg

Banana Macadamia Nut Bread

Bake this flavorful banana bread for a festive breakfast or brunch.

Preparation time: 20 minutes
Baking time: 35 minutes

[3 mini loaves; 8 servings/loaf]

2	cups all-purpose flour
3/4	cup sugar
1/2	cup LAND O LAKES® Butter, softened
2	eggs
1	tablespoon grated orange zest
1	teaspoon baking soda
1	teaspoon vanilla
1/2	teaspoon salt
2	medium (1 cup) ripe bananas, mashed
1/4	cup orange juice
1	cup flaked coconut
1	(3 1/2-ounce) jar (3/4 cup) coarsely chopped macadamia nuts

1. Heat oven to 350°. Combine all ingredients *except* bananas, orange juice, coconut and nuts in large mixer bowl. Beat at low speed, scraping bowl often, until well mixed (2 to 3 minutes).

2. Add bananas and orange juice. Continue beating, scraping bowl often, until well mixed (1 minute). Stir in coconut and nuts by hand. (Batter will be thick.)

3. Spread into three greased (5 1/2x3-inch) mini loaf pans. Bake for 35 to 45 minutes or until toothpick inserted in center comes out clean. Cool 10 minutes; remove from pans. Cool completely.

Nutrition Facts (1 serving): Calories 160; Protein 2 g; Carbohydrate 19 g; Dietary Fiber 0 g; Fat 9 g; Cholesterol 30 mg; Sodium 140 mg

TIP This bread can also be baked in one greased (9x5-inch) loaf pan. Bake for 60 to 65 minutes or until toothpick inserted in center comes out clean. Cool 10 minutes; remove from pan. Cool completely.

[kitchen notes]

The zest or outer peel of citrus fruits contains aromatic and highly flavorful oils that add both color and flavor to many recipes. To properly "zest" an orange, lemon or lime, use a zester, which has five tiny round holes on its cutting surface, or a small grater. Grate only down to the white membrane or pith, which has a bitter flavor.

Apricot Cream Coffee Cake

Apricot preserves and a lemon glaze top this rich cream cheese coffee cake.

Preparation time: 20 minutes
Baking time: 45 minutes
Cooling time: 20 minutes

[16 servings]

COFFEE CAKE

1¾ cups all-purpose flour
½ cup sugar
¾ cup LAND O LAKES® Butter, softened
2 eggs
½ teaspoon baking powder
½ teaspoon baking soda
¼ teaspoon salt
1 teaspoon vanilla

FILLING

¼ cup sugar
1 (8-ounce) package cream cheese, softened
1 egg
1 teaspoon grated lemon zest
1 (10-ounce) jar apricot preserves

GLAZE

⅓ cup powdered sugar
2-3 teaspoons lemon juice

1. Heat oven to 350°. Grease and flour bottom and sides of 10-inch springform pan.

2. Combine all coffee cake ingredients in large mixer bowl. Beat at medium speed, scraping bowl often, until well mixed (1 to 2 minutes). Spread batter on bottom and 2 inches up sides of prepared pan.

3. Combine all filling ingredients *except* apricot preserves in small mixer bowl. Beat at medium speed, scraping bowl often, until smooth (2 to 3 minutes). Pour over batter in pan. Spoon preserves evenly over filling.

4. Bake for 45 to 55 minutes or until crust is golden brown. Cool 20 minutes. Loosen sides of cake from pan by running knife around inside of pan; remove side of pan.

5. Meanwhile, stir together powdered sugar and lemon juice in small bowl until smooth. Drizzle over warm coffee cake. Serve warm or cold; store refrigerated.

Nutrition Facts (1 serving): Calories 280; Protein 4 g; Carbohydrate 35 g; Dietary Fiber 0 g; Fat 15 g; Cholesterol 80 mg; Sodium 220 mg

Pepper Cheese Beer Bread

A flavorful soup is the perfect accompaniment for this spicy cheese-infused bread.

Preparation time: 15 minutes
Baking time: 45 minutes

[1 loaf; 12 servings]

1 cup all-purpose flour
1 cup whole wheat flour
6 ounces (1½ cups) LAND O LAKES® Hot Pepper Monterey Jack Cheese, shredded
1 teaspoon sugar
¾ teaspoon baking powder
½ teaspoon baking soda
½ teaspoon salt
1 cup beer
⅓ cup LAND O LAKES® Butter, melted
2 eggs, slightly beaten

1. Heat oven to 350°. Stir together flour, whole wheat flour, *1 cup* cheese, sugar, baking powder, baking soda and salt in medium bowl. Stir in beer, butter and eggs just until moistened.

2. Spoon batter into greased 9x5-inch loaf pan. Sprinkle remaining cheese over top of batter.

3. Bake for 45 to 55 minutes or until toothpick inserted in center comes out clean. Cool 10 minutes; remove from pan. Serve warm.

Nutrition Facts (1 serving): Calories 190; Protein 7 g; Carbohydrate 17 g; Dietary Fiber 2 g; Fat 11 g; Cholesterol 65 mg; Sodium 310 mg

TIP When baking with beer, bring it to room temperature before using for best results.

Apricot Cream Coffee Cake

Cheddar Pecan Bread

Cheese, chives and pecans flavor a recipe that's delicious served warm or cold.

Preparation time: 30 minutes
Rising time: 1 hour 45 minutes
Baking time: 40 minutes

[2 loaves; 12 servings/loaf]

2	(¼-ounce) packages active dry yeast
2	cups warm water (105° to 115°F)
1	tablespoon sugar
1	cup coarsely chopped pecans
½-¾	cup chopped fresh chives*
¼	cup LAND O LAKES® Butter, softened
¼	cup honey
12	ounces (3 cups) LAND O LAKES® Cheddar Cheese, shredded
2	teaspoons salt
5½-6½	cups bread flour *or* all-purpose flour

1. Dissolve yeast in warm water in small bowl. Stir in sugar; let stand 5 minutes.

2. Meanwhile, combine pecans, chives, butter, honey, cheese and salt in large mixer bowl. Add yeast mixture and *3 cups* flour to cheese mixture. Beat at medium speed, scraping bowl often, until smooth (2 to 3 minutes). Stir in enough remaining flour by hand to make dough easy to handle. Cover; let stand 10 minutes.

3. Turn dough onto lightly floured surface; knead until smooth and elastic (8 to 10 minutes). Place in greased bowl; turn greased-side up. Cover; let rise in warm place until double in size (about 1 hour). (Dough is ready if indentation remains when touched.)

4. Punch down dough; divide in half. Shape each half into loaf. Place loaves in two greased (9x5-inch) loaf pans. Cover; let rise in warm place until double in size (about 45 minutes).

5. *Heat oven to 375°.* Bake for 40 to 45 minutes or until loaves sound hollow when tapped. If tops of loaves are browning too quickly, cover loosely with aluminum foil during last 10 minutes of baking. Remove from pans immediately.

Nutrition Facts (1 serving): Calories 240; Protein 8 g; Carbohydrate 28 g; Dietary Fiber 1 g; Fat 11 g; Cholesterol 20 mg; Sodium 290 mg

*Substitute ¼ cup dried chives.

Three Grain Whole Wheat Bread

This bread machine recipe is made with both rye and whole wheat.

Preparation time: 15 minutes
Processing time: 4 hours

[1½-pound loaf; 12 servings]
[2-pound loaf; 16 servings]

1½-POUND LOAF

1¼	cups water
1	tablespoon LAND O LAKES® Butter, softened
2	tablespoons nonfat dry milk
1	teaspoon salt
3	tablespoons firmly packed brown sugar
1	cup whole wheat flour
1½	cups bread flour
½	cup rye flour
1½	teaspoons active dry yeast

2-POUND LOAF

1½	cups water
1½	tablespoons LAND O LAKES® Butter, softened
3	tablespoons nonfat dry milk
1¼	teaspoons salt
¼	cup firmly packed brown sugar
1½	cups whole wheat flour
1¾	cups bread flour
¾	cup rye flour
2	teaspoons active dry yeast

1. Select loaf size setting and follow proper loaf size measurements. Prepare bread according to bread machine manual instructions.

Nutrition Facts (1 serving; 1½-pound loaf): Calories 80; Protein 2 g; Carbohydrate 16 g; Dietary Fiber 2 g; Fat 1.5 g; Cholesterol 5 mg; Sodium 190 mg

Almost as comforting as the result itself is the aroma that fills the kitchen when this coffee cake bakes.

Raisin 'n Nut Pull-Apart Coffee Cake

Perfect for a potluck or family gathering, this timeless pull-apart bread will serve a crowd.

Preparation time: 1 hour
Rising time: 2 hours 15 minutes
Baking time: 35 minutes

[1 coffee cake; 24 servings]

COFFEE CAKE

1	cup milk
¼	cup LAND O LAKES® Butter
1	(¼-ounce) package active dry yeast
¼	cup warm water (105° to 115°F)
3½-4	cups all-purpose flour
¼	cup sugar
1	egg
½	teaspoon salt

FILLING

1	cup sugar
½	cup chopped pecans
1½	teaspoons ground cinnamon
½	cup LAND O LAKES® Butter, melted
½	cup golden raisins

1. Heat milk in 1-quart saucepan over medium heat until it just comes to a boil (5 to 7 minutes). Stir in ¼ cup butter until melted. Cool to warm (105° to 115°F).

2. Dissolve yeast in warm water in large mixer bowl. Add cooled milk mixture, *2 cups* flour, ¼ cup sugar, egg and salt. Beat at medium speed, scraping bowl often, until smooth (1 to 2 minutes). Stir in enough remaining flour by hand to make dough easy to handle.

3. Turn dough onto lightly floured surface; knead until smooth and elastic (about 10 minutes). Place in greased bowl; turn greased-side up. Cover; let rise in warm place until double in size (about 1½ hours). (Dough is ready if indentation remains when touched.)

4. Punch down dough; divide in half. Shape each half with floured hands into 24 balls. Stir together 1 cup sugar, pecans and cinnamon in small bowl. Dip balls first in melted butter, then in sugar mixture. Place 12 balls in bottom of greased 10 inch tube pan or Bundt® pan. (If using removable bottom tube pan, line with aluminum foil.) Sprinkle with raisins. Top with remaining 12 balls. Cover; let rise until double in size (about 45 minutes).

5. *Heat oven to 375°.* Bake for 35 to 40 minutes or until coffee cake sounds hollow when tapped. (Cover with aluminum foil if coffee cake browns too quickly.) Immediately invert pan on heatproof serving plate. Let stand 1 minute to allow sugar mixture to drizzle over cake. Remove pan; serve warm.

Nutrition Facts (1 serving): Calories 190; Protein 3 g; Carbohydrate 28 g; Dietary Fiber 0 g; Fat 8 g; Cholesterol 25 mg; Sodium 110 mg

Gingersnap Mini Muffins

These tiny ginger muffins are delicious with marmalade or plain as a bite-size snack.

Preparation time: 25 minutes
Baking time: 11 minutes

[4 dozen mini muffins]

¼	cup sugar
¼	cup firmly packed brown sugar
½	cup LAND O LAKES® Butter, softened
⅔	cup light molasses
1	egg
1½	teaspoons baking soda
1	teaspoon ground cinnamon
1	teaspoon ground ginger
½	teaspoon ground cloves
2	teaspoons grated lemon zest
2½	cups all-purpose flour
1	cup LAND O LAKES® Light *or* Fat Free Sour Cream

Powdered sugar
Orange marmalade

1. Heat oven to 375°. Combine all muffin ingredients *except* flour, sour cream, powdered sugar and orange marmalade in large mixer bowl. Beat at medium speed until well mixed (2 to 3 minutes). Add flour and sour cream; continue beating until well mixed (1 to 2 minutes).

2. Spoon batter into greased mini muffin pans, filling cups ¾ full. Bake for 11 to 14 minutes or until toothpick inserted in center comes out clean. Let stand 5 minutes; remove from pans. Sprinkle with powdered sugar; serve with orange marmalade.

Nutrition Facts (3 mini muffins): Calories 210; Protein 3 g; Carbohydrate 32 g; Dietary Fiber 0 g; Fat 8 g; Cholesterol 17 mg; Sodium 190 mg

TIP For standard size muffins, use a 12-cup muffin pan and bake for 14 to 18 minutes. Makes 2½ dozen muffins.

Prize-Winning Blueberry Muffins

A hint of fresh lemon zest adds a special flavor to these scrumptious muffins.

Preparation time: 20 minutes
Baking time: 20 minutes

[1 dozen muffins]

½	cup sugar
¼	cup LAND O LAKES® Butter, softened
1	cup LAND O LAKES® Sour Cream
1	egg
2	tablespoons lemon juice
1½	teaspoons grated lemon zest
1½	cups all-purpose flour
1	teaspoon baking soda
1	cup fresh or frozen blueberries (unthawed)
1	tablespoon sugar
½	teaspoon grated lemon zest

1. Heat oven to 375°. Combine ½ cup sugar and butter in large mixer bowl. Beat at medium speed, scraping bowl often, until creamy (1 to 2 minutes). Add sour cream, egg, lemon juice and 1½ teaspoons lemon zest. Continue beating, scraping bowl often, until well mixed (1 to 2 minutes).

2. Stir together flour and baking soda in medium bowl. Stir flour mixture into sour cream mixture by hand just until moistened. Gently stir in blueberries.

3. Spoon batter into greased or paper-lined muffin pan. Stir together 1 tablespoon sugar and ½ teaspoon lemon zest in small bowl. Sprinkle about ¼ teaspoon mixture on top of each muffin. Bake for 20 to 25 minutes or until lightly browned. Cool 5 minutes; remove from pan.

Nutrition Facts (1 muffin): Calories 170; Protein 4 g; Carbohydrate 26 g; Dietary Fiber 0 g; Fat 6 g; Cholesterol 50 mg; Sodium 170 mg

Gingersnap Mini Muffins

Apple-Nut Coffee Cake

Perfect for a weekend brunch, this coffee cake is a Land O'Lakes classic.

Preparation time: 20 minutes
Baking time: 30 minutes

[15 servings]

CAKE

2	cups all-purpose flour
1	cup sugar
½	cup LAND O LAKES® Sour Cream
½	cup LAND O LAKES® Butter, softened
¼	cup milk
2	eggs
1	teaspoon baking powder
1	teaspoon baking soda
1	teaspoon vanilla
¼	teaspoon salt
2	medium (2 cups) cooking apples, peeled, chopped*

TOPPING

½	cup chopped walnuts *or* pecans
½	cup firmly packed brown sugar
2	tablespoons LAND O LAKES® Butter, melted
1	teaspoon ground cinnamon

1. Heat oven to 350°. Combine all cake ingredients *except* apples in large mixer bowl. Beat at medium speed, scraping bowl often, until smooth (2 to 3 minutes). Gently stir in apples by hand.

2. Spread batter into greased 13x9-inch baking pan. Combine all topping ingredients in small bowl; sprinkle over batter.

3. Bake for 30 to 35 minutes or until toothpick inserted in center comes out clean.

Nutrition Facts (1 serving): Calories 270; Protein 4 g; Carbohydrate 37 g; Dietary Fiber 1 g; Fat 13 g; Cholesterol 55 mg; Sodium 250 mg

*Substitute 1 (16-ounce) can peaches, drained, chopped.

TIP We recommend using Red Rome, Winesap, McIntosh or Haralson apples.

Potato Chive Bread

Use chives fresh from the garden in this aromatic and unusual bread.

Preparation time: 20 minutes
Processing time: 4 hours

[1½-pound loaf; 12 servings]
[2-pound loaf; 18 servings]

1½-POUND LOAF

½	cup water
½	cup chopped unpeeled potatoes
3	tablespoons LAND O LAKES® Butter
1¼	cups buttermilk
1	teaspoon salt
2½	cups bread flour
½	cup whole wheat flour
¼	cup chopped fresh chives*
1	tablespoon sugar
2	teaspoons active dry yeast

2-POUND LOAF

½	cup water
⅔	cup chopped unpeeled potatoes
3	tablespoons LAND O LAKES® Butter
1¼	cups buttermilk
1½	teaspoons salt
3	cups bread flour
½	cup whole wheat flour
¼	cup chopped fresh chives*
2	tablespoons sugar
2	tablespoons active dry yeast

1. Bring water to a full boil in small saucepan; add potatoes. Cook over high heat until potatoes are almost fork tender (about 6 minutes). Add butter. Cook until butter is melted and potatoes are fork-tender (1 to 2 minutes). Add buttermilk to potato mixture to equal 1⅓ cups.

2. Select loaf size setting and follow proper loaf size measurements. Prepare bread according to bread machine manual instructions.

Nutrition Facts (1 serving; 1½-pound loaf): Calories 70; Protein 2 g; Carbohydrate 9 g; Dietary Fiber 1 g; Fat 3 g; Cholesterol 10 mg; Sodium 210 mg

*Substitute 2 tablespoons dried chives.

Pumpkin Banana Chocolate Chip Bread

Three favorite flavors are combined in this moist and delicious bread.

Preparation time: 20 minutes
Baking time: 40 minutes

[5 mini loaves; 8 servings/loaf]

1½   cups firmly packed brown sugar
¾   cup LAND O LAKES® Butter, softened
3   eggs
1   cup cooked pumpkin
2   medium (1 cup) ripe bananas, mashed
3   cups all-purpose flour
2   teaspoons baking soda
1½   teaspoons pumpkin pie spice*
½   teaspoon baking powder
½   teaspoon salt
½   cup miniature semi-sweet chocolate chips**

1. Heat oven to 350°. Combine brown sugar, butter and eggs in large mixer bowl. Beat at medium speed, scraping bowl often, until mixture is creamy (1 to 2 minutes).

2. Add pumpkin and bananas. Continue beating until well mixed (1 to 2 minutes). (Mixture will have curdled appearance.) Add all remaining ingredients *except* chocolate chips. Continue beating just until moistened (about 1 minute). Stir in chocolate chips by hand.

3. Spread into five greased (5½x3-inch) mini loaf pans. Bake for 40 to 50 minutes or until toothpick inserted in center comes out clean. Cool 5 minutes; remove from pans. Cool completely.

Nutrition Facts (1 serving): Calories 150; Protein 2 g; Carbohydrate 23 g; Dietary Fiber 0 g; Fat 6 g; Cholesterol 30 mg; Sodium 160 mg

*Substitute ¾ teaspoon ground cinnamon, ½ teaspoon ground ginger, ¼ teaspoon *each* ground nutmeg and ground cloves.

**Substitute ½ cup semi-sweet chocolate chips.

TIP This bread can also be baked in one greased (9x5-inch) loaf pan. Bake for 65 to 75 minutes or until toothpick inserted in center comes out clean. Cool 5 minutes; remove from pan. Cool completely.

[kitchen notes]

The best banana bread is made with slightly over-ripe bananas.
But you can't always plan to have them on hand—and when you do, you
may not be in a position to bake. Here's a quick tip to improve your timing and
your bread: buy bananas, let them ripen, and then freeze. When you're ready
to bake, simply thaw at room temperature for several hours, and mash as usual.

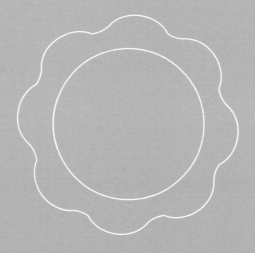

Sweet Comforts

Somehow, a little bit of sugar reinforces our contentment when all's right with the world and likewise soothes us when the blues strike. Sit, relax, savor the wonderfully blended flavors and textures of Caramel Apple Pie, Old-Fashioned Bread Pudding and more traditional homestyle desserts.

Caramel Apple Pie

Technique

No matter how modest, every dessert tastes better when you use the best ingredients available. Use freshly squeezed lemon juice, for example, and ripe fruit in season. Always choose real chocolate, butter and vanilla extract over imitations.

Wash fresh fruit just before using to preserve its texture. Berries are especially fragile and must be rinsed gently.

To save time, chop nuts and measure and mix dry ingredients ahead of time. You can even make your own cake or quick bread "mixes" by combining dry ingredients for a given recipe; place in a resealable plastic food bag, label and use within two months for best results.

Caramel Apple Pie

This decadent pie is a flavorful ending to a cold-weather supper.

Preparation time: 40 minutes
Baking time: 55 minutes
Cooling time: 30 minutes

[8 servings]

PASTRY

2	cups all-purpose flour
¼	teaspoon salt
⅔	cup cold LAND O LAKES® Butter
4-5	tablespoons cold water
1	tablespoon LAND O LAKES® Butter, melted
1	teaspoon sugar

FILLING

¼	cup thick caramel ice cream topping
6	medium (6 cups) tart cooking apples, peeled, sliced ¼-inch
1	tablespoon lemon juice
½	cup sugar
¼	cup firmly packed brown sugar
¼	cup all-purpose flour
1	teaspoon ground cinnamon

1. Heat oven to 400°. Stir together 2 cups flour and salt in large bowl; cut in butter until crumbly. Mix in water with fork until flour is just moistened.

2. Divide pastry in half; shape each half into a ball. Wrap 1 ball in plastic food wrap; refrigerate.

3. Roll out remaining pastry ball on lightly floured surface into 12-inch circle. Place in 9-inch pie pan. Trim pastry to ½ inch from rim of pan. Set aside.

4. Lightly toss together ice cream topping, apples and lemon juice in large bowl. Add ½ cup sugar, brown sugar, ¼ cup flour and cinnamon; toss lightly. Spoon apple mixture into prepared crust.

5. Roll remaining pastry ball into 11-inch circle. Cut out 10 (½-inch) strips with sharp knife or pastry wheel. Place five strips, 1 inch apart, across filling in pie pan. Weave remaining five strips at right angles to strips already in place. Trim ends. Fold trimmed edge of bottom pastry over strips; build up an edge. Crimp or flute edge. Brush strips with 1 tablespoon melted butter; sprinkle with 1 teaspoon sugar. Cover edge of crust with 2-inch strip aluminum foil.

6. Bake for 35 minutes. Remove aluminum foil. Continue baking for 20 to 25 minutes or until crust is lightly browned and juice begins to bubble through slits in crust. Cool pie 30 to 45 minutes. Serve warm.

Nutrition Facts (1 serving): Calories 440; Protein 5 g; Carbohydrate 70 g; Dietary Fiber 1 g; Fat 17 g; Cholesterol 45 mg; Sodium 280 mg

Pumpkin Gingerbread

Pumpkin, molasses and spices combine for a moist and distinctive gingerbread.

Preparation time: 15 minutes
Baking time: 38 minutes
Cooling time: 10 minutes

[9 servings]

GINGERBREAD

1¾ cups all-purpose flour
1½ teaspoons ground ginger
1 teaspoon baking powder
1 teaspoon baking soda
1 teaspoon ground cinnamon
½ teaspoon salt
½ teaspoon ground nutmeg
½ teaspoon ground cloves
¾ cup cooked pumpkin
½ cup firmly packed brown sugar
½ cup LAND O LAKES® Butter, softened
½ cup molasses
1 egg

FROSTING

½ cup firmly packed brown sugar
½ cup LAND O LAKES® Butter
½ cup flaked coconut
½ cup chopped pecans

1. Heat oven to 350°. Combine flour, ginger, baking powder, baking soda, cinnamon, salt, nutmeg and cloves in medium bowl. Set aside.

2. Combine pumpkin, ½ cup brown sugar, ½ cup butter, molasses and egg in large bowl. Beat at medium speed, scraping bowl often, until creamy (1 to 2 minutes). Reduce speed to low; add flour mixture. Beat until well mixed (1 to 2 minutes).

3. Spoon into greased and floured 8-inch square baking pan. Bake for 38 to 43 minutes or until toothpick inserted in center comes out clean. Cool 10 minutes.

4. Meanwhile, combine ½ cup brown sugar and ½ cup butter in small saucepan. Cook over medium heat, stirring occasionally, until mixture comes to a boil. Continue cooking 1 minute. Stir in coconut and pecans. Spoon evenly over warm gingerbread. Serve warm or cool.

Nutrition Facts (1 serving): Calories 490; Protein 4 g; Carbohydrate 60 g; Dietary Fiber 2 g; Fat 27 g; Cholesterol 80 mg; Sodium 560 mg

[kitchen notes]

The inclusion of molasses in any gingerbread recipe
helps to give this distinctive treat its trademark color, flavor and texture.
In baking, it is fine to use either light or dark unsulfured molasses
to enhance flavors. We do not recommend using blackstrap molasses,
which is somewhat bitter and may overpower more delicate spices.

Orange Nut Butter Cake

Use your favorite nut in this brunch or coffee offering.

Preparation time: 30 minutes
Baking time: 50 minutes
Cooling time: 1 hour

[16 servings]

CAKE

1	cup sugar
3/4	cup LAND O LAKES® Butter, softened
3	eggs
1	tablespoon grated orange zest
1	teaspoon vanilla
1	cup orange marmalade
3	cups all-purpose flour
1	teaspoon baking soda
1/2	teaspoon baking powder
1/2	teaspoon salt
1/3	cup orange juice
1	(5-ounce) can evaporated milk
1	cup chopped nuts

GLAZE

1	cup powdered sugar
1	tablespoon LAND O LAKES® Butter, softened
1/2	teaspoon grated orange zest
2-3	tablespoons orange juice

1. Heat oven to 350°. Combine sugar and 3/4 cup butter in large mixer bowl. Beat at medium speed, scraping bowl often, until creamy (1 to 2 minutes). Continue beating, adding eggs one at a time, beating well after each addition until well mixed (1 to 2 minutes). Reduce speed to low; add orange zest, vanilla and orange marmalade. Beat until well mixed (1 to 2 minutes).

2. Combine flour, baking soda, baking powder and salt in medium bowl. Gradually add flour mixture alternately with orange juice and evaporated milk to butter mixture until well mixed (1 to 2 minutes). Stir in chopped nuts by hand.

3. Spoon into greased and floured 10-inch tube pan. Bake for 50 to 60 minutes or until toothpick inserted in center comes out clean. Cool in pan 10 minutes; remove from pan. Cool completely.

4. Combine all glaze ingredients *except* orange juice in small mixer bowl. Beat at low speed, scraping bowl often and gradually adding enough orange juice for desired glazing consistency. Glaze cooled cake.

Nutrition Facts (1 serving): Calories 370; Protein 6 g; Carbohydrate 54 g; Dietary Fiber 1 g; Fat 16 g; Cholesterol 70 mg; Sodium 280 mg

Old-Fashioned Bread Pudding With Vanilla Sauce

This traditional vanilla- and nutmeg-infused bread pudding is topped with a velvety smooth sauce.

Preparation time: 15 minutes
Baking time: 40 minutes

[8 servings]

PUDDING

4	cups (8 slices) cubed white bread
1/2	cup raisins
2	cups milk
1/4	cup LAND O LAKES® Butter
1/2	cup sugar
2	eggs, slightly beaten
1	teaspoon vanilla
1/2	teaspoon ground nutmeg

SAUCE

1/2	cup LAND O LAKES® Butter
1/2	cup sugar
1/2	cup firmly packed brown sugar
1/2	cup whipping cream
1	teaspoon vanilla

1. Heat oven to 350°. Combine bread and raisins in large bowl. Combine milk and 1/4 cup butter in 1-quart saucepan. Cook over medium heat until butter is melted (4 to 7 minutes). Pour milk mixture over bread; let stand 10 minutes.

2. Stir in all remaining pudding ingredients. Pour into greased 1 1/2-quart casserole. Bake for 40 to 50 minutes or until set in center.

3. Combine all sauce ingredients *except* vanilla in 1-quart saucepan. Cook over medium heat, stirring occasionally, until mixture thickens and comes to a full boil (5 to 8 minutes). Stir in vanilla.

4. To serve, spoon warm pudding into individual dessert dishes; serve with sauce. Store refrigerated.

Nutrition Facts (1 serving): Calories 470; Protein 6 g; Carbohydrate 56 g; Dietary Fiber 1 g; Fat 26 g; Cholesterol 125 mg; Sodium 310 mg

Cool and creamy, this layered icebox cake is a diner dessert-case classic—just the thing for a midnight snack.

Icebox Banana Cake with Chocolate Cream

This cake tastes great from the refrigerator or freezes beautifully for a chilled treat.

Preparation time: 1 hour
Baking time: 20 minutes
Cooling time: 30 minutes
Chilling time: 2 hours

[12 servings]

CAKE

1	cup sugar
⅔	cup LAND O LAKES® Butter, softened
2	teaspoons vanilla
2	eggs
2	medium (1 cup) ripe bananas, mashed
¼	cup LAND O LAKES® Sour Cream
1½	cups all-purpose flour
1	teaspoon baking soda

CHOCOLATE CREAM

1½	cups chilled whipping cream
3	tablespoons powdered sugar
1	teaspoon vanilla
½	cup semi-sweet real chocolate chips, melted
2	bananas
2	tablespoons chopped pecans

1. Heat oven to 350°. Combine sugar, butter and 2 teaspoons vanilla in large mixer bowl. Beat at low speed, scraping bowl often, until creamy (1 to 2 minutes). Continue beating, adding eggs one at a time, until well mixed. Stir in 1 cup mashed bananas and sour cream by hand. Gently stir in flour and baking soda.

2. Pour into two greased and floured (9-inch) round cake pans. Bake for 20 to 25 minutes or until toothpick inserted in center comes out clean. Cool 5 minutes; remove from pans. Cool completely.

3. Beat chilled whipping cream at high speed in chilled small mixer bowl, scraping bowl often, until soft peaks form (1 to 2 minutes).

Continue beating, gradually adding sugar and 1 teaspoon vanilla, until stiff peaks form (1 to 2 minutes). Add melted chocolate. Continue beating until well mixed (1 minute). (DO NOT OVER-BEAT.)

4. Place one cake layer on serving plate; spread with *half* of chocolate cream. Slice one banana; lay banana slices on top of chocolate cream. Top with remaining cake layer. Frost top of cake with remaining chocolate cream. Cover; refrigerate 2 hours or overnight.

5. Just before serving, slice remaining banana; arrange banana slices around outside edge of cake. Sprinkle pecans in center of cake. Store refrigerated.

Nutrition Facts (1 serving): Calories 420; Protein 4 g; Carbohydrate 45 g; Dietary Fiber 1 g; Fat 26 g; Cholesterol 110 mg; Sodium 220 mg

TIP This cake can also be baked in two (8-inch) round cake pans. Bake for 25 to 30 minutes.

Brownie Macaroon Pudding Cake

Rich with coconut and chocolate syrup, this cake almost calls for a spoon.

Preparation time: 15 minutes
Baking time: 32 minutes

[9 servings]

1	cup all-purpose flour
¾	cup sugar
¼	cup unsweetened cocoa
1	tablespoon baking powder
½	teaspoon salt
½	cup milk
3	tablespoons LAND O LAKES® Butter, melted
1	teaspoon vanilla
1	cup flaked coconut
1	cup hot water
½	cup chocolate syrup

1. Heat oven to 350°. Combine flour, sugar, cocoa, baking powder and salt in medium bowl. Add milk, butter and vanilla; mix well until smooth. Stir in coconut.

2. Spread batter into greased 8-inch square baking dish. Combine hot water and chocolate syrup in 2-cup glass measure. Pour evenly over batter.

3. Bake for 32 to 38 minutes or until center is set and edges pull away from sides of pan. Serve warm.

Nutrition Facts (1 serving): Calories 250; Protein 3 g; Carbohydrate 45 g; Dietary Fiber 2 g; Fat 8 g; Cholesterol 10 mg; Sodium 370 mg

Lemon Cream Cheesecake

Impress family and friends with this rich, citrusy dessert.

Preparation time: 45 minutes
Baking time: 8 minutes
Chilling time: 3 hours 45 minutes

[12 servings]

CRUST

1	cup (about 25) crushed vanilla wafers
2	tablespoons LAND O LAKES® Butter, melted

FILLING

1	cup lemon juice
¼	cup water
2	(¼-ounce) envelopes unflavored gelatin
1½	cups sugar
5	eggs, slightly beaten
1	tablespoon grated lemon zest
½	cup LAND O LAKES® Butter, softened
2	(8-ounce) packages cream cheese, softened
½	cup chilled whipping cream

Sweetened whipped cream, if desired
Lemon slices, if desired

1. Heat oven to 375°. Stir together all crust ingredients in small bowl. Press on bottom of 9-inch springform pan. Bake for 8 to 10 minutes until lightly browned; cool.

2. Meanwhile, combine lemon juice and water in 2-quart saucepan; sprinkle with gelatin. Let stand 5 minutes to soften. Add sugar, eggs and lemon zest. Cook over medium heat, stirring constantly, until mixture just comes to a boil (8 to 10 minutes). (DO NOT BOIL.)

3. Combine ½ cup butter and cream cheese in large mixer bowl. Beat at medium speed, scraping bowl often, until well mixed (1 to 2 minutes). Gradually beat in hot lemon mixture until well mixed (1 to 2 minutes). Refrigerate, stirring occasionally, until cool (about 45 minutes).

4. Beat ½ cup whipping cream in chilled small mixer bowl at high speed, scraping bowl often, until soft peaks form (1 to 2 minutes). Gently stir into lemon mixture.

5. Pour into prepared crust. Cover; refrigerate until firm (3 to 4 hours).

6. Loosen edge of cheesecake with knife; remove side of pan. Garnish top of cheesecake with whipped cream and lemon slices.

Nutrition Facts (1 serving): Calories 430; Protein 7 g; Carbohydrate 34 g; Dietary Fiber 0 g; Fat 30 g; Cholesterol 170 mg; Sodium 270 mg

Brownie Macaroon Pudding Cake

Ginger Lemonade Cookies

The zest of lemon meets the tang of ginger in this lightly glazed cookie.

Preparation time: 1 hour
Baking time: 12 minutes

[4½ dozen cookies]

COOKIE

¾ cup sugar
¾ cup LAND O LAKES® Butter, softened
2 eggs
2½ cups all-purpose flour
½ cup frozen lemonade concentrate
2 teaspoons ground ginger
½ teaspoon baking soda
¼ teaspoon salt

GLAZE

½ cup powdered sugar
2 tablespoons frozen lemonade concentrate

1. Heat oven to 375°. Combine sugar, butter and eggs in large mixer bowl. Beat at medium speed, scraping bowl often, until creamy (1 to 2 minutes). Reduce speed to low; add all remaining cookie ingredients. Beat until well mixed (1 to 2 minutes).

2. Drop dough by rounded teaspoonfuls onto ungreased cookie sheets. Bake for 12 to 14 minutes or until lightly browned.

3. Meanwhile, stir together powdered sugar and 2 tablespoons frozen lemonade concentrate in small bowl until smooth. Drizzle warm cookies with glaze.

Nutrition Facts (1 cookie): Calories 70; Protein 1 g; Carbohydrate 10 g; Dietary Fiber 0 g; Fat 3 g; Cholesterol 15 mg; Sodium 50 mg

Sour Cream Cherry Pie

Meringue tops a rich sour cream pie made with sweet dried cherries.

Preparation time: 30 minutes
Baking time: 52 minutes
Cooling time: 30 minutes
Chilling time: 1 hour

[8 servings]

PASTRY

Single-crust unbaked 9-inch pie pastry

FILLING

1 cup dried cherries
3 egg yolks
2 cups LAND O LAKES® Sour Cream
1 cup firmly packed brown sugar
2 tablespoons all-purpose flour
1 teaspoon almond extract

MERINGUE

3 egg whites
½ teaspoon cream of tartar
⅓ cup sugar
½ teaspoon almond extract

1. Heat oven to 425°. Place cherries in medium bowl; pour enough boiling water over cherries to cover. Let stand for 5 minutes.

2. Meanwhile, beat egg yolks in large mixer bowl until thick and lemon-colored (3 to 4 minutes). Stir in sour cream, brown sugar, flour and 1 teaspoon extract. Beat at medium speed, scraping bowl often, until well mixed (1 to 2 minutes). Stir in cherries by hand.

3. Place pastry in 9-inch pie plate. Crimp or flute edge. Pour filling into prepared pastry. Bake for 20 minutes. *Reduce oven to 350°.* Continue baking for 20 minutes.

4. Meanwhile, beat egg whites and cream of tartar in large mixer bowl until frothy. Continue beating, gradually adding ⅓ cup sugar, until stiff peaks form and mixture is glossy (3 to 4 minutes). Spread meringue over filling, sealing meringue to crust edge and mounding slightly in center. Bake for 12 to 15 minutes or until meringue is lightly browned.

5. Cool to room temperature (30 to 40 minutes). Refrigerate at least 1 hour before serving. Store refrigerated.

Nutrition Facts (1 serving): Calories 460; Protein 7 g; Carbohydrate 63 g; Dietary Fiber 1 g; Fat 21 g; Cholesterol 115 mg; Sodium 190 mg

Red Devil's Food Cake

Fluffy, cooked vanilla frosting showcases this classic chocolate cake.

Preparation time: 45 minutes
Baking time: 35 minutes
Cooling time: 1 hour

[15 servings]

CAKE

2¼ cups cake flour
½ cup unsweetened cocoa
1 teaspoon baking soda
½ teaspoon salt
1½ cups sugar
¾ cup LAND O LAKES® Butter, softened
1 (1-ounce) bottle red food color
2 eggs
2 teaspoons vanilla
1 cup buttermilk
1 teaspoon vinegar

FROSTING

⅔ cup milk
2 tablespoons all-purpose flour
¼ teaspoon salt
⅔ cup sugar
⅔ cup LAND O LAKES® Butter, softened
½ teaspoon vanilla

1. Heat oven to 350°. Stir together cake flour, cocoa, baking soda and salt in medium bowl. Set aside.

2. Combine 1½ cups sugar and ¾ cup butter in large mixer bowl. Beat at medium speed, scraping bowl often, until creamy (1 to 2 minutes). Add food color, eggs and vanilla; mix well (1 to 2 minutes). Continue beating, gradually adding flour mixture with buttermilk and vinegar and scraping bowl often, until well mixed (1 to 2 minutes).

3. Pour cake batter into greased 13x9-inch baking pan. Bake for 35 to 40 minutes or until toothpick inserted in center comes out clean. Cool 10 minutes. Remove from pans. Cool completely.

4. Meanwhile, combine milk, flour and salt in 1-quart saucepan. Cook over medium heat, stirring constantly, until mixture thickens and comes to a boil (4 to 6 minutes). Boil 1 minute. Cover surface with plastic wrap; cool completely (1 hour).

5. Beat ⅔ cup sugar, ⅔ cup butter and ½ teaspoon vanilla in large mixer bowl at medium speed, scraping bowl often, until creamy (1 to 2 minutes). Gradually add cooled flour mixture. Beat at medium speed, scraping bowl often, until light and fluffy (4 to 5 minutes). Frost cooled cake.

Nutrition Facts (1 serving): Calories 370; Protein 5 g; Carbohydrate 47 g; Dietary Fiber 2 g; Fat 19 g; Cholesterol 75 mg; Sodium 590 mg

---

[kitchen notes]

This classic American cake, made with dark chocolate, takes its name from its sinfully rich texture and flavor, although the association is clearly made with humor. The first devil's food recipe appeared in 1905, its dark color in marked contrast to the snowy white of angel food cake, an earlier confection.

Orange Date Cookies

These old-fashioned date cookies are accented with orange peel and a buttery orange frosting.

Preparation time: 1 hour
Baking time: 12 minutes

[3½ dozen cookies]

COOKIE

¾	cup LAND O LAKES® Butter
½	cup sugar
¼	cup water
1	(8-ounce) package chopped dates
2	cups all-purpose flour
1	cup chopped pecans
¼	cup orange juice
1	egg
1	tablespoon grated orange zest
½	teaspoon baking powder
½	teaspoon salt
¼	teaspoon baking soda

FROSTING

2	cups powdered sugar
¼	cup LAND O LAKES® Butter, softened
1	tablespoon grated orange zest
2-3	tablespoons orange juice

1. Heat oven to 350°. Combine ¾ cup butter, sugar, water and dates in 3-quart saucepan. Cook over low heat, stirring constantly, until dates are softened (5 to 8 minutes). Remove from heat; cool 15 minutes.

2. Stir in all remaining cookie ingredients by hand until well mixed.

3. Drop dough by tablespoonfuls 2 inches apart onto ungreased cookie sheets. Bake for 12 to 14 minutes or until edges are lightly browned. Cool completely.

4. Combine all frosting ingredients *except* orange juice in small mixer bowl. Beat at low speed, scraping bowl often and gradually adding enough orange juice for desired spreading consistency. Frost cooled cookies.

Nutrition Facts (1 cookie): Calories 130; Protein 1 g; Carbohydrate 17 g; Dietary Fiber 1 g; Fat 6 g; Cholesterol 15 mg; Sodium 80 mg

Chocolate Almond Silk Pie

Rich and decadent, this silk pie blends the flavors of toasted almond and chocolate.

Preparation time: 20 minutes
Baking time: 8 minutes
Cooling time: 30 minutes
Chilling time: 3 hours

[8 servings]

PASTRY

1	cup all-purpose flour
¼	cup finely chopped toasted almonds
6	tablespoons LAND O LAKES® Butter, softened
3	tablespoons powdered sugar
¼	teaspoon vanilla

FILLING

1	cup sugar
¾	cup LAND O LAKES® Butter, softened
3	(1-ounce) squares unsweetened chocolate, melted, cooled
¾	cup pasteurized refrigerated egg substitute
½	teaspoon almond extract

Sweetened whipped cream, if desired
Toasted sliced almonds, if desired

1. Heat oven to 400°. Combine all crust ingredients in small mixer bowl. Beat at low speed, scraping bowl often, until well mixed (2 to 3 minutes).

2. Press onto bottom and up sides of 9-inch pie pan. Bake for 8 to 10 minutes or until lightly browned. Cool completely.

3. Meanwhile, combine sugar, ¾ cup butter and chocolate in small mixer bowl. Beat at medium speed, scraping bowl often, until creamy (2 to 3 minutes). Continue beating, gradually adding egg substitute and almond extract and scraping bowl often, until well mixed (2 to 3 minutes). Spoon mixture into cooled crust. Refrigerate until firm (3 to 4 hours).

4. Dollop with whipped cream; sprinkle with almonds, if desired.

Nutrition Facts (1 serving): Calories 500; Protein 6 g; Carbohydrate 44 g; Dietary Fiber 3 g; Fat 36 g; Cholesterol 150 mg; Sodium 290 mg

Orange Date Cookies

Brown Sugar-Iced Applesauce Bars

This moist applesauce bar is glazed with a mixture of butter and brown sugar.

Preparation time: 30 minutes
Baking time: 24 minutes
Cooling time: 30 minutes

[60 bars]

BAR
1   cup sugar
¾   cup LAND O LAKES® Butter, softened
2   cups thick and chunky applesauce
1   egg
1   teaspoon vanilla
2½ cups all-purpose flour
2   teaspoons baking soda
½   teaspoon salt
½   teaspoon ground cinnamon
1   cup raisins
1   cup chopped walnuts

FROSTING
½   cup LAND O LAKES® Butter
1   cup firmly packed brown sugar
⅛   teaspoon salt
¼   cup milk
1   teaspoon vanilla
2¾ cups powdered sugar

1. Heat oven to 350°. Combine sugar and ¾ cup butter in large mixer bowl. Beat at medium speed, scraping bowl often, until well mixed (1 to 2 minutes). Add applesauce, egg and 1 teaspoon vanilla. Continue beating until well mixed (1 to 2 minutes).

2. Reduce speed to low. Add flour, baking soda, ½ teaspoon salt and cinnamon. Beat until well mixed (1 to 2 minutes). Stir in raisins and walnuts by hand.

3. Pour into greased 15x10x1-inch jelly-roll pan. Bake for 24 to 28 minutes or until golden brown. Cool completely.

4. Meanwhile, melt ½ cup butter in 2-quart saucepan; stir in brown sugar and ⅛ teaspoon salt. Cook over medium heat until mixture comes to a boil (3 to 5 minutes). Reduce heat to low. Cook, stirring occasionally, 2 minutes. Remove from heat. Carefully stir in milk. Cook over medium heat, stirring occasionally, 1 minute. Remove from heat. Stir in vanilla.

5. Beat with wire whisk, gradually adding powdered sugar until mixture is smooth (2 to 3 minutes). Frost cooled bars immediately; cut into bars.

Nutrition Facts (1 bar): Calories 130; Protein 1 g; Carbohydrate 20 g; Dietary Fiber 0 g; Fat 5 g; Cholesterol 15 mg; Sodium 105 mg

TIP Work quickly when frosting bars. If frosting thickens, add milk, 1 tablespoon at a time.

Vanilla Crazy Cake

Make and bake this cake in a single pan; enjoy it in less than an hour.

Preparation time: 15 minutes
Baking time: 30 minutes

[9 servings]

1¼ cups all-purpose flour
1   cup sugar
1½ teaspoons baking powder
½   teaspoon salt
1   egg
1   teaspoon vanilla
⅓   cup vegetable oil
¾   cup milk
¼   cup chopped pecans

½   cup semi-sweet real chocolate chips

1. Heat oven to 350°. Combine flour, sugar, baking powder and salt in 8-inch square baking pan. Set aside.

2. Stir together egg and vanilla in small bowl with wire whisk. Make *2* indentations in flour mixture; pour oil in one and egg mixture in other. Pour milk over flour mixture; mix well. Stir in pecans.

3. Bake for 30 to 40 minutes or until toothpick inserted in center comes out clean. Sprinkle chocolate chips over warm cake. Let stand 2 minutes; slightly swirl melted chips.

Nutrition Facts (1 serving): Calories 310; Protein 4 g; Carbohydrate 43 g; Dietary Fiber 1 g; Fat 14 g; Cholesterol 25 mg; Sodium 220 mg

What's another word for comfort? Chocolate—and never has it been better than in this double-decker cake layered with light and dark buttercream frosting.

Fudge Cake with Chocolate Buttercream Frosting

For a truly special ending to a family gathering, serve generous slices of this chocolate masterpiece.

Preparation time: 30 minutes
Baking time: 30 minutes
Cooling time: 1 hour 15 minutes

[16 servings]

CAKE

1¼	cups sugar
1	cup LAND O LAKES® Butter, softened
3	(1-ounce) squares unsweetened baking chocolate, melted, cooled
2	teaspoons vanilla
3	eggs
2	cups all-purpose flour
1	teaspoon baking soda
¼	teaspoon salt
1	cup buttermilk

FROSTING

¾	cup LAND O LAKES® Butter, softened
5	cups powdered sugar
⅓	cup whipping cream
1	teaspoon vanilla
2	tablespoons light corn syrup
2	(1-ounce) squares unsweetened baking chocolate, melted, cooled

1. Heat oven to 350°. Combine sugar and 1 cup butter in large mixer bowl. Beat at medium speed, scraping bowl often, until creamy (1 to 2 minutes). Add cooled chocolate and vanilla. Continue beating, scraping bowl often, until well mixed (1 minute). Continue beating, adding eggs 1 at a time, until well mixed (1 to 2 minutes). Reduce speed to low. Beat, gradually adding flour, baking soda and salt alternately with buttermilk and scraping bowl often, until well mixed (1 to 2 minutes).

2. Pour into two greased and floured (9-inch) round cake pans. Bake for 30 to 40 minutes or until toothpick inserted in center comes out clean.

3. Cool 15 minutes; remove from pans. Cool completely.

4. Meanwhile, beat ¾ cup butter in large mixer bowl at medium speed until creamy (1 to 2 minutes). Continue beating, gradually adding powdered sugar alternately with whipping cream and vanilla and scraping bowl often, until light and fluffy (1 to 2 minutes). Add corn syrup; mix well. *Reserve ½ cup frosting for cake filling.*

5. Add melted unsweetened baking chocolate to remaining frosting; mix well.

6. Place 1 cake layer on serving plate; spread top with reserved frosting. Top with remaining cake layer; frost top and sides with chocolate frosting.

Nutrition Facts (1 serving): Calories 540; Protein 4 g; Carbohydrate 71 g; Dietary Fiber 2 g; Fat 28 g; Cholesterol 100 mg; Sodium 350 mg

TIP If frosting is too thin, beat in additional powdered sugar.

Chocolate Swirl Sour Cream Cake

Marbled with a rich fudge sauce, this yellow cake is perfect for a festive family gathering.

Preparation time: 45 minutes
Baking time: 40 minutes
Cooling time: 1 hour

[15 servings]

CAKE

2⅓	cups all-purpose flour
1½	cups sugar
1	cup LAND O LAKES® Sour Cream
¾	cup milk
½	cup LAND O LAKES® Butter, softened
1	teaspoon baking soda
1	teaspoon salt
½	teaspoon baking powder
2	eggs
1	teaspoon vanilla
½	cup hot fudge ice cream topping

FROSTING

12	ounces (2 cups) real milk chocolate chips
1	cup LAND O LAKES® Sour Cream
½	teaspoon vanilla

1. Heat oven to 350°. Combine all cake ingredients *except* hot fudge topping in large mixer bowl. Beat at medium speed, scraping bowl often, until well mixed (2 to 3 minutes). *Reserve ½ cup cake batter; set aside.* Spread remaining batter into greased 13x9-inch baking pan.

2. Stir together reserved ½ cup cake batter and ½ cup hot fudge topping in small bowl. Drop mixture by spoonfuls evenly over batter. Pull knife through batter for marbled effect. Bake for 40 to 50 minutes or until top springs back when touched lightly in center. Cool completely.

3. Melt milk chocolate chips in 1-quart saucepan over medium heat, stirring constantly, until smooth (2 to 3 minutes). Place melted chocolate in small mixer bowl. Add 1 cup sour cream and ½ teaspoon vanilla. Beat at medium speed, scraping bowl often, until smooth and creamy (1 to 2 minutes). Frost cooled cake.

Nutrition Facts (1 serving): Calories 410; Protein 7 g; Carbohydrate 58 g; Dietary Fiber 0 g; Fat 18 g; Cholesterol 60 mg; Sodium 360 mg

Cheesecake Dessert Squares

Rich and creamy cheesecake bars are a popular choice for a casual dessert.

Preparation time: 10 minutes
Baking time: 20 minutes
Cooling time: 30 minutes
Chilling time: 4 hours

[15 servings]

CRUST

1¾	cups graham cracker crumbs
6	tablespoons LAND O LAKES® Butter, melted
3	tablespoons sugar

FILLING

1	cup sugar
2	(8-ounce) packages cream cheese, softened
4	eggs, beaten
1	(21-ounce) can blueberry pie filling

1. Heat oven to 375°. Combine all crust ingredients in medium bowl; mix well. Press firmly on bottom of 13x9-inch baking pan. Set aside.

2. Combine 1 cup sugar, cream cheese and eggs in large mixer bowl. Beat at medium speed, scraping bowl often, until smooth (2 to 3 minutes).

3. Pour filling into prepared crust. Bake for 20 to 25 minutes or until firm. Cool completely.

4. Spread pie filling carefully over top of cheesecake. Cover; refrigerate until firm (at least 4 hours).

Nutrition Facts (1 serving): Calories 330; Protein 5 g; Carbohydrate 38 g; Dietary Fiber 1 g; Fat 18 g; Cholesterol 100 mg; Sodium 250 mg

Chocolate Swirl Sour Cream Cake

Index